Kathryn R. Blackstone is Lecturer in Religious Studies at Victoria University of Wellington.

WOMEN IN THE FOOTSTEPS OF THE BUDDHA

Women in the Footsteps of the Buddha

Struggle for Liberation in the Therīgāthā

KATHRYN R. BLACKSTONE

MOTILAL BANARSIDASS PUBLISHERS
PRIVATE LIMITED • DELHI

First Indian Edition: Delhi, 2000
First Published: Britain, 1998

Published in association with
Curzon Press, Britain

Extracts from K.R. Norman's translation of the *Theragātha* and *Therīgāthā* are reproduced with the kind permission of the Pali Text Society

ISBN: 81-208-1715-x

Also available at:

MOTILAL BANARSIDASS
236, 9th Main III Block, Jayanagar, Bangalore 560 001
41 U.A. Bungalow Road, Jawahar Nagar, Delhi 110 007
8 Mahalaxmi Chamber, Warden Road, Mumbai 400 026
120 Royapettah High Road, Mylapore, Chennai 600 004
Sanas Plaza, 1302, Baji Rao Road, Pune 411 002
8 Camac Street, Calcutta 700 017
Ashok Rajpath, Patna 800 004
Chowk, Varanasi 221 001

British Library Cataloguing in Publication Data
A catalogue record of this book is available from the British Library

FOR SALE IN SOUTH ASIA ONLY

Printed in India
BY JAINENDRA PRAKASH JAIN AT SHRI JAINENDRA PRESS,
A-45 NARAINA, PHASE I, NEW DELHI 110 028
AND PUBLISHED BY NARENDRA PRAKASH JAIN FOR
MOTILAL BANARSIDASS PUBLISHERS PRIVATE LIMITED,
BUNGALOW ROAD, DELHI 110 007

For Glen Harper, with love and thanks for making my own struggle so much easier ... and more fun.

CONTENTS

EDITORS' PREFACE

In recent years the academic study of Buddhism in the West has grown in exciting new directions. To be sure, the vast panorama of Buddhism has become more available to modern scholars, but Buddhist Studies has also attracted an ever-increasing group of serious, interested scholars who have brought to their inquiries a wonderful variety of new pursuits and methodologies, invigorating the discipline as never before. While scholars are continually opening new arenas for dialogue, such as the Buddhist movement in the West, the relationship of Buddhism and human rights, socially engaged Buddhism, and a veritable plethora of other stimulating topics, many of the traditional Buddhist texts are also benefitting from renewed attention.

The *Therīgāthā* is one such text. Susan Murcott's *The First Buddhist Women: Translations and Commentary of the Therīgāthā* (Berkeley: Parallax Press, 1991) was one of the first new studies of this important Pali Buddhist classic. Interesting scholarly articles, too, such as Kevin Trainor's important 'In the Eye of the Beholder: Nonattachment and the Body in Subhā's Verse (*Therīgāthā* 71),' published in the *Journal of the American Academy of Religion* [61 (1993): 57–79], have begun to appear with regularity. Kathryn Blackstone's *Women in the Footsteps of the Buddha: Struggle for Liberation in the Therīgāthā* is a most important addition to this literature.

Beginning from the presumption that the *Therīgāthā* is a most 'exciting and provocative text,' Kathryn Blackstone goes far beyond the traditional exploration of the text as an expression of the attainment of Buddhism's early women renunciants.

Without losing any sense of the intense beauty and dramatic value of the poems, she coaxes us into an detailed exploration of the quest for liberation on the part of the early *bhikkunīs*. She considers this issue not only on the basis of previous historical studies, and informed by the complicated symbolism of the text, but also in order to unearth the attitudes and assumptions inherent in the text, and to examine the terms, images, events, and situations insofar as they reveal the feminine perspective of the *bhikkhunī-sangha*.

Blackstone moves beyond her predescessors in that she offers *both* a qualitative and quantitative analysis of the text, compared throughout to its companion text, the *Theragāthā*. Her analyses show that while the two texts employ identical form, structure, and style, their utilization of terms, phrases, stock descriptions, and stylistic devices reflect important differences in emphasis. Her careful analysis of the language and imagery of the texts allows her to postulate some bold new conclusions about the text, supported by an interesting compilation of data, presented in four appendixes.

In light of the above, the Curzon Critical Studies in Buddhism is delighted to present this important new study.

PREFACE

This monograph is a revision of my M.A. thesis, originally researched and written at McMaster University, 1989–1990. The focus and methodology of the thesis evolved in a context of converstation and friendly argument with four special people: Pat Dold who convinced me to let a text speak for itself, even if what it says contradicts my expectations; Mavis Fenn who steered me to the *Therīgāthā* and *Theragāthā* in response to my questions about how Buddhist renunciants understand *nibbāna*; Anne Pearson who showed me the importance of discovering women's own perspective on their religion and the strength and courage they maintain, even in seemingly oppressive systems; and Graeme MacQueen who encouraged me to push myself beyond 'doctrinal interpretations,' suggested that I count terms, and then helped me translate mathematics into English prose. With their help, advice, and willingness to argue with me, my work and my experience as a graduate student have been greatly enriched.

Their influence is very evident throughout my work. My study consists almost entirely of a close reading of the *Therīgāthā* and the *Theragāthā*. Other sources (commentarial, canonical and scholarly) were consulted only after I had grappled with the issues in the texts themselves. I have tried not to presuppose definitions of key terms, situations, and patterns of expression, but have sought to discover how the authors of the texts understood them. Finally, I have maintained a clear focus on the specifically feminine perspective claimed by the *Therīgāthā*. I use the *Theragāthā* only to establish how the *Therīgāthā*'s perspective is distinctive.

When I began researching, I was surprised and appalled by how little serious scholarship there has been on the texts. This lacuna remains, even after a gap of five years. This is particularly surprising in the case of the *Therīgāthā* which is unique in its focus on female religious experience and its claim to female authorship. So, although I was somewhat ambivalent about publishing my M.A. thesis, when Charles Prebish asked me to include it in his series, I accepted. I can only hope my work will encourage further research by those who are better equipped to address the textual, historical, and sociological issues I could only glimpse when I wrote the thesis.

I am very aware of its shortcomings, in particular, my use of translations. When I wrote the thesis, I was just beginning to develop my language skills. When I revised it, I did not have the time to provide my own translations of the texts. Throughout the following study, I present K.R. Norman's translations of *Elders' Verses* I and II, though I have consulted the Pali extensively.

I also fear that the numerical approach I utilize in analyzing the texts interferes with the beauty of some of the poems. To compensate for this, I open each chapter with a quote from C.A.F. Rhys Davids' translations to poetically evoke the sentiment I discuss in the chapter.

As the chapter titles and section headings indicate, this study is designed to discover the distinctive perspective of the *Therīgāthā*. My own perspective has been shaped by many influences. Though they are too numerous to name, I would like to thank all my friends for their support over the years, especially Pat Dold, who showed the thesis to Charles Prebish, and who is, therefore, responsible for this publication. I also thank Ellen Badone, David Kinsley, and Graeme MacQueen for comments on the thesis, and Marilyn Nefsky, Keith Parry, Eileen Schuller, and Adele Reinhartz for helping me refine my skills in research, analysis, and presentation. To Mandy Bergland I extend my heartfelt appreciation for generously sharing her technical expertise (and computer!) with me. Charles Prebish I thank for patient and encouraging editorial assistance. I would also like to thank my students for listening attentively to my stories from the *Therīgāthā* and for asking me thought-provoking questions that clarified my thinking.

The thesis and revisions were written under the financial support of an Ontario Graduate Scholarship (1989–90) and a Social Sciences and Humanities Research Council of Canada Doctoral Fellowship (1990–94), for which I am very grateful. A portion of this monograph was presented at the Canadian Society for the Study of Religion (May, 1991).

Finally, I extend my deepest gratitude to my family who have cheerfully endured the trials of graduate work and the stresses of writing a book. Thanks to Kyra and Zach for making me play when I needed to, and to Harp for covering my share of the housework, making me explain myself clearly, and never giving up faith in me and my work.

INTRODUCTION

The *Therīgāthā*: Text and Context

> Now the Order of *Bhikkhunīs* being thus well established, and multiplying in diverse villages, towns, country districts, and royal residences, dames, daughters-in-law and maidens of the clans, hearing of the great enlightenment of the Buddha, of the very truth of the Norm, of the excellent practices of the Order, were mightily pleased with the system, and, dreading the round of rebirth, they sought permission of husband, parents, and kin, and taking the system to their bosom, renounced the world. So renouncing and living virtuously, they received instruction from the Master and the Elders, and with toil and effort soon realized Arahant-ship. And the psalms which they uttered from time to time, in bursts of enthusiasm and otherwise, were afterwards by the Recensionists included in the Rehearsal, and arranged together in eleven cantos. They are called the Verses of the Elder Women...
>
> Dhammapāla, *Paramatthadīpanī*[1]

The *Therīgāthā* is an exciting and provocative text. As far as I know, it is the only canonical text in the world's religions that is attributed to female authorship and that focuses exclusively on women's religious experiences.[2] In the specific context of Buddhism, it stands as a unique testimony to the experiences and aspirations of the community of women renunciants, the *bhikkhunī-sangha*. As such, it is important both for scholars interested in the history and doctrine of Indian Buddhism and to contemporary Buddhist women seeking liberative models from the past. Furthermore, as interest in the influence of gender on religious texts, institutions, and practices has developed over recent years, the *Therīgāthā* has become central to studies of women in Buddhism and to the history of women in ancient India.[3]

These are important reasons for engaging in a detailed analysis of the text. Even without them, however, the text would be worthy of study. Quite simply, the text contains great stories. Some of the poems in the collection are beautifully constructed, humorous, and emotionally powerful, even in translation. Others, of course, are rather arid, but the collection as a whole is intrinsically interesting. When I have retold the stories in the collection to friends, colleagues, and undergraduate classes, they have never failed to elicit a response. One does not need to be a scholar, a Buddhist, or a feminist to appreciate the stories and to be moved by the emotions they evoke. Currently in Sri Lanka, the story of Paṭācārā (*Therīgāthā* 112–116) has been made into a film[4] and Subhā Jīvakambavanikā's gift of her eye to the rogue who was accosting her is the subject of a popular song (*Therīgāthā* 366–399).[5]

I am interested in all the levels of possible interpretation of the text. As a feminist scholar of Buddhism, I am fascinated by the text's presentation of women's religiosity and its claim to female authorship. My specific interests in Buddhism also find a venue in the text. The text's focus on liberation (*nibbāna*, the religious goal of early Buddhism) fits in nicely with my long-standing interest in Buddhist soteriology. And, I have always been drawn to stories as an effective, if not the most effective, means of conveying religious truths.

The *Therīgāthā* thus presents me with an ideal subject. However, the study of this text, like all other texts in the Pali Canon, is not a simple task. We simply cannot know with any certainty the dating, authorship, or geographical location in which the text was composed. Though tradition maintains that all the texts of the Pali Canon were transcribed into written form in the first century B.C.E. in Sri Lanka, the earliest date we can identify for the *Therīgāthā* is the sixth century, with

Dhammapāla's commentary on the text, the *Paramatthadīpanī*. Yet even this date is misleading, as Dhammapāla was working from an extant manuscript.

There is also a very high probability that the text was transmitted orally for hundreds of years prior to its transcription. Several scholars have noted this, and K.R. Norman concludes that it was composed over a three hundred year period from the late sixth to the end of the third centuries.[6] The oral origins of the written text make analysis even more difficult. Not only are we uncertain about authorship, geographical location, and exact date of composition, but the long period of oral preservation means that the original utterances would inevitably become modified as generations of reciters memorized and performed the poems.

Scholars of oral narrative generally agree that the transmission of stories is a process in which both adaptation and preservation occur. Most scholars also agree the particular features of a story that are preserved or adapted are determined by the complex relationship between the performer, the audience, and the ideological context in which it is told. Narrative convention also plays a role, as, in order to be remembered and appreciated, the story must conform with traditional patterns of expression.[7] Thus, oral narratives are, in some ways, as representative of the social context in which they are told as they are of the personality of the performer and the narrative tradition they express.

There is little doubt that the *Therīgāthā* is a highly formalized text that conforms very closely with an established tradition of verse-composition. One need only glance through the text and its companion volume, the *Theragāthā*, to find overwhelming evidence of rigid conventionalism.

The *Therīgāthā* and *Theragāthā* are collections of verses compiled into poems[8] ascribed to the earliest followers of the Buddha, female and male, respectively. Both collections are arranged by ascending number of verses per poem, from shortest to longest. The *Therīgāthā* is thus a collection of five hundred twenty-two verses compiled into seventy-three poems.

The *Theragāthā* has one thousand two hundred seventy-nine verses arranged in two hundred sixty-four poems. All the poems in both collections are ascribed to specific people, but the actual authorship of the poems is impossible to ascertain. Many of the poems are addressed to or are about their ascribed authors and three of the poems in the *Therīgāthā* have their author unnamed (1, 23, 67).[9] Although many of the longer poems are carefully crafted as coherent units, others are obviously compilations with various fragments joined together somewhat arbitrarily. And, as K.R. Norman points out, at the time of compilation some verses explaining the circumstances of the poem's utterance were added by the redactor(s).[10]

Thus, we cannot know if the *therīs* and *theras* to whom the poems are ascribed actually composed the verses or if they ever uttered them. However, the structure of the poems does provide an indication of the method by which they were constructed. The verses in both collections are very repetitive.[11] The identical terms, phrases, and whole *pādas* used in the poems indicate the presence of a large pool of refrains and phrases that was available to the *bhikkhunīs* and *bhikkhus*. K.R. Norman thinks it likely that 'some of these verses and *pādas* are very old, perhaps older than Buddhism, for they are found also in Jain and Brahmanical literature.'[12] Anyone who so desired could choose appropriate verses from this pool and construct a unified poem from the pieces.

Some of the poems are very beautiful and dramatic compositions. In his study of Pali metre, A.K. Warder distinguishes Subhā Jīvakambavanikā's poem (*Therīgāthā*, 366–399) as a particuarly good example of lyric poetry that appears to have been performed as a dramatic production resembling, but ante-dating classical Sanskrit drama.[13] The entertainment value of some of the longer poems is very high – even in translation, they continue to evoke humour, sadness, and joy.

Further, the poems are not only entertaining, they are also educational. The major emphasis of the poems is the quest for liberation. Both texts are devoted almost entirely to descriptions of liberation, methods to attain it, or characteristics of those individuals who have attained it. All the authors of both collections are described by the commentary as having attained liberation, i.e., as having become *arahants*.[14] These 'devotional' sections that comprise the vast majority of repeated phrases and verses are juxtaposed with poetic accounts of the situation, setting, and emotional state of the ascribed authors.

In a comparative study of Prakrit poetry and the *Therīgāthā* and *Theragāthā*, Siegfried Lienhard points out the difference between the more 'poetic' segments of the poems and the devotional, or 'Buddhist' segments.[15] This study provides considerable evidence of a borrowing of poetic motifs and composition styles from secular poetry. Again we see the method by which the poems were constructed. The authors[16] could select situations and motifs from secular and devotional poetry, constructing their compositions by uniting the various elements together. These constructions serve the dual purpose of entertaining and educating simultaneously.

These features of the texts' construction and content provide us with a hint of a possible reason for the texts' preservation. Their educational and entertainment value are given additional credibility by the status of the ascribed authors, the foremost of the earliest *bhikkhunīs* and *bhikkhus*. The poems of the *Therīgāthā* and *Theragāthā* are not only beautiful, devotional, and instructive, they are also reputed to be the records of the experiences of the Buddha's first followers, all of whom are accredited with *arahanthood*. Furthermore, as Étienne Lamotte reports, the Buddha is recorded to voice his approval of chanted verses (in this case, the *theras*' verses):

> Excellent, excellent, O monk! You have a fine voice, well articulated, neither muffled nor gulped, and which makes the meaning clearly understandable.[17]

Dhammapāla's commentary further emphasizes the status of the ascribed authors by frequently alluding to the *sutta* in which the Buddha categorized all his followers according to their special abilities.[18] Though many of the verses are addressed to or are about the *therīs* and *theras* to whom they are ascribed, the association between the poems and famous *bhikkhunīs* or *bhikkhus* imbues the poems with the weight of a traditional veneration for those individuals thought worthy by the Buddha.

Thus, we can easily imagine that the early *sangha* had a high regard for the verses and poems. These features help us understand how the texts survived a long period of oral preservation. The metre, repetitiveness and emotional power of the poems could help reciters' memories, and the high status of the *arahant* authors would provide the motivation for recitation, preservation, and eventual transcription.

I think there is also another reason for the texts' preservation. The texts are unique in the Pali Canon as descriptions of the quest for liberation of the Buddha's followers. The Buddha is a relatively frequent character in the verses, but they are not primarily about him. Rather, they detail the path to liberation followed by the foremost of his disciples. As such, I think they fulfil the purpose of 'liberation manuals', that is, they function as models of the successful quest for liberation that anyone can follow. This hypothesis opens up exciting possibilities for the interpretation of the *Therīgāthā*. If the poems in the text do indeed function as models of success, we can interpret them as symbols that reflect communal values and preoccupations.

Almost all scholars studying symbolism follow Clifford Geertz's classic insight that symbols both reflect and shape the world in which we live. Symbols function both as 'models of' our social and ideological world and as 'models for' what we think that world should be.[19] More recently, the linguistic analysis of George Lakoff and Mark Johnson extends this theory into the realm of language. Language, as a complex symbol system, both expresses and influences our conceptual understanding of the world, thereby defining and delimiting our perceptions of 'reality'.[20]

In Lakoff and Johnson's theory, the symbols we use and the language with which we express ourselves are closely associated with our experiences. For example, if our usual mode of transportation is bus, we might speak metaphorically of time in terms of waiting at a bus stop in the rain. If we drive, we would probably use metaphors of red lights or traffic jams. Although both types of metaphors are embedded in our culture and are readily understandable to people from our culture, our particular experience and our assessment our audience's experience will determine our choice of metaphor.

These theories provide a useful array of methods for the analysis of religious literature, particularly, as in the case of the *Therīgāthā*, where we can detect a didactic function. The terms and images employed by the authors are not arbitrary, but are clearly designed to communicate certain religious truths. A study of these terms and images can thus enable us to glimpse the symbolic universe the authors inhabit and wish to convey.[21]

In my study of the *Therīgāthā*, I apply this theory of symbolism to the text. I treat the text holistically as the product of communal values and conventions. If, as I think is probable, the text did indeed function as a collection of models of the successful quest, a close examination of those models can tell us a lot about what the *bhikkhunīs* thought important in their choice to pursue a religious vocation.[22]

My goal in the following chapters is to uncover the attitudes and assumptions that underly the *Therīgāthā*'s characteristic use of terms, images, events, and situations. I am interested in the specifically feminine perspective the text claims to reflect. This cannot be accomplished with a study of the text in isolation; there must be a basis for comparison. The *Theragāthā* as a companion volume that is almost identical in vocabulary, style, and structure, but which claims male authorship, is a convenient text by which to establish the distinctiveness of the *Therīgāthā*.

My study is thus comprised of a comparative analysis of the terms, images, and situations presented in the *Therīgāthā* and *Theragāthā*. The analysis is both quantitative and qualitative. I have calculated and compared the frequency of occurrence of words, phrases, images, and stock descriptions in each text. In my study, I draw upon and present K.R. Norman's translations,[23] though I have consulted the Pali extensively.[24] In the Appendices, I provide extensive tables of the verses in which the terms, phrases, images, and situations occur. I have also devoted considerable attention to the context in which these terms, phrases, and descriptions are placed, the speaker whom the text claims to have uttered them, and variations in thematic emphasis they appear to represent.

The qualitative analysis involves an assessment of the prevailing themes or patterns of expression that are revealed by differences in the texts' characteristic usage of identical terms, phrases, stock descriptions, and stylistic devices. My argument here is that although the texts are remarkably similar – they are identical in form, structure, and style – they nonetheless exhibit consistent differences in emphasis.

My close analysis of the language and imagery used by the texts can enable us to identify clearly the preoccupations and assumptions that characterize both their similarities and their differences. It can also help us to confirm the probability of female authorship of the *Therīgāthā*. The frequency of occurrence of terms, phrases, and situations is easily verifiable and, one may assume, indicates something of the relative value placed upon them. The qualitative analysis is, of course, more subjective, but the consistency with which each text maintains its thematic emphasis is hard to refute.

My focus, however, is firmly on the *Therīgāthā*. I use the *Theragāthā* only for the purposes of comparison. I make no attempt to present a balanced discussion of the two texts. The themes I explore are those that are prominent in the *Therīgāthā*, and not necessarily the *Theragāthā*. Discussions throughout my study frequently involve an assessment of what the *Therīgāthā* is in contrast with what the *Theragāthā* is not. I do not intend this in any way to be construed as representative of the *Theragāthā*. If I had focused on the *Theragāthā*, the discussion would have been slanted the other way – it would have stressed what the *Theragāthā* is, and the *Therīgāthā* is not.

My study is thus designed to reveal gender differences between the texts. As recent feminist scholarship has shown, gender can play an important role in both the experiences and the modes of expression typical of women and men in a given social system. Studies have documented how women and men tend to tell different types of stories, emphasise different components of the stories, and respond differently to stories.[25]

The work of Caroline Walker Bynum is particularly pertinent to my study as she investigates the influence of gender on the use of religious imagery in the biographies of medieval Christian female saints. By comparing the model of women's religiosity in these biographies with those of contemporary male saints, Bynum demonstrates how social, psychological, and religious conceptions of gender influence the ways women understand and express their religiosity.[26] Her main contention is that all persons work within the constraints of their social and religious milieu in interpreting and expressing their religious experiences. This milieu presents different types of contraints and opportunities for women than for men. Because women and men have thereby encountered differing expectations and requisites of what is considered to be a religious lifestyle, gender differences pervade their religious expressions.

This insight and the comparative methodology underlying it are supported by my research on the *Therīgāthā* and the *Theragāthā*. There is little doubt that Buddhism has maintained a clear distinction between women and men throughout its history.[27] The socio-religious milieu in which Buddhism arose and developed in ancient India was almost certainly patriarchal. All the religious literature generally considered to be contemporary with the formative period of Buddhism contain passages that advocate or assume women's subordination to men, in both the secular and religious realms. Perhaps the most striking example of this is Manu's explicit condemnation of a woman's autonomy at any time in her life:

> She should do nothing independently, even in her own house.
>
> In childhood subject to her father, in youth to her husband, and when her husband is dead to her sons, she should never enjoy independence... Though [her husband] be uncouth and prone to pleasure, though he has no good

points at all, the virtuous wife should ever worship her lord as a god.[28]

As we shall see in the following chapters, Buddhist literature also condemns women's independence, and the *Vinaya* rules for *bhikkhunīs* insist on their formal subordination to *bhikkhus* in all matters of monastic life.[29]

Jain texts also contain numerous passages that reflect patriarchal assumptions about women's inherent nature and appropriately subordinate role in society and religious community. In Jain texts, however, as in no other corpus of religious literature, the issues of how this inherent nature affects women's soteriological capacity are actively debated. Early in its history, Jainism split into two branches, the Śvetāmbara and the Digambara, the former of which acknowledges women's capacity to attain *mokṣa*, while the latter does not. The issue of women's soteriological capacity comprises the basis of a series of debates, compiled and translated recently by Padmanabh Jaini.[30]

This patriarchal context makes the *Therīgāthā*'s claim to female authorship all the more remarkable. Buddhist texts also maintain a consistently patriarchal and androcentric attitude towards women. Throughout my study, I discuss specific aspects of Buddhist patriarchy as they are relevant to the topic examined in each chapter. My main focus, however, is not the relationship between the texts and the rest of the canon in which they are included. Rather, I am interested in identifying and comparing the perspective towards central elements of Buddhist doctrine assumed by each text. I establish the influence of gender in particularly important texts throughout the Pali Canon to demonstrate both that the texts are part of the same tradition and that the androcentric assumptions maintained throughout the canon are reflected in the texts' specific perspective.

Throughout the following study, I accept the traditional claim to female authorship of the *Therīgāthā*, though my argument for doing so will have to wait until the conclusion where I compile the results of my study. I think the assumptions of gender differences that pervade Buddhist literature had an inevitable affect on the religious expressions of members of the Buddhist community of renunciants. Though we cannot prove conclusively that the texts were composed by women and men, we can establish that they reflect a differing perspective that conforms closely with what we would expect of women and men immersed in a patriarchal environment.

The title of this monograph thus employs a pun on the term 'liberation'. My central focus in the following chapters is literally 'liberation': in the Buddhist sense of the term as *nibbāna*, liberation from the cycle of *saṃsāra* and the suffering concommitant with it; and, in the feminist sense, as women's liberation from gender constraints and the oppression they bring. To the modern reader, this may seem anachronistic, as though a twentieth century concept were being imposed upon an ancient text, but the *Therīgāthā* bears witness to the claim of feminist scholars that women have a history of independent thought and action. Though the text is far from a feminist rebellion against sex discrimination, it does relate the experiences and perceptions of a group of female renunciants who engaged in an alternate lifestyle that 'liberated' them to some extent from the gender expectations of their social world. In this way, the *Therīgāthā* provides us all, Buddhists and feminists alike, with a model of women's persistent and effective struggle for liberation.

CHAPTER I

The Language of Liberation

As we would listen to the call of distant lions' roar Resounding from the hollow of the hills, Listen to the verses of them whose selves were trained, Telling us messages about themselves: How they were named, and what their kin, and how They kept the Faith, and how they found Release. Wise and unfaltering they lived their lives; Now here, now there they saw the Vision gleam; They reached, they touched the ageless, deathless Way; And retrospective of the accomplished End, They set to speech these matters of their quest.

Dhammapāla, *Paramatthadīpanī*[1]

According to Pali textual sources, the religious goal of early Buddhism was *nibbāna*, liberation from the cycle of *saṃsāra*.[2] The Buddha's attainment of *nibbāna* is the culminating event in all his biographies, and the quest for this goal comprises the main import of his teachings. The life of renunciation and the *Vinaya* rules that circumscribe it are designed to propel people towards that goal. The goal, in short, is the definitive religious characteristic of Buddhism.

Nibbāna is frequently defined as the utterly transformative realization of the impermanence of all things, and the concomitant severing of the bonds of *saṃsāra*, the relentless cycle of desire, attachment, delusion, animosity, and grief to which human beings are bound. To realize the truth of impermanence and the insubstantiality of all things is to liberate oneself from bondage to one's mistaken expectations and perceptions of value. *Nibbāna* involves a thorough transformation of human cognitive and emotive faculties, including prevailing attitude, ways of interacting with others, and the structure of one's perceptions of reality. In metaphoric terms, *nibbāna* means the obliteration of one's socially conditioned lenses, so that one no longer perceives things through a filter, but sees things 'as they really are'. This shattering, the 'blowing-out' of false, desire-ridden perceptions, results in an emotional state of absolute equanimity. One is no longer at the mercy of unrealistic expectations, of one's ceaseless striving for stability in the midst of relentless waves of change. Instead, in truly understanding the absolute pervasiveness of change, one accepts whatever happens as a natural consequence of what has come before; one achieves a state of perfect peace.

As the opening quote from Dhammapāla's commentary indicates, the main emphasis of the *Therīgāthā* and *Theragāthā* is the quest for this ultimate religious goal. Both texts are devoted almost entirely to descriptions of liberation, methods to attain it, or characteristics of those individuals who have attained it. It is the most frequently referred to, the most frequently symbolized, and the clear goal of most of the authors. All the authors of both collections are described by the commentary as having attained liberation, that is, as having become *arahants*.

In this way, the texts are similar to the *Jātakas* or the *Apadānas*. Moreover, their preoccupation with the experiences of the ascribed authors in a single lifetime marks them as quite distinct. The Buddha is frequently referred to, particularly in the *Theragāthā*, but the verses, for the most part, are not about him. Rather, they focus on the quest for liberation of his followers. However, unlike the *Apadānas*, they are not overly concerned with the past lives of the authors and the karmic events that led to their attainment of *nibbāna*. They thus appear to be 'liberation manuals' designed to provide models of success for the women and men who join the Buddhist *sangha*.

The *Therīgāthā* and *Theragāthā* employ two mediums to explain the meaning of *nibbāna* and to convey the authors' attainment of it. The vast majority of the verses contain highly formalized technical terms that are common throughout Buddhist and even Jain *gāthās*.[3] Many of the verses also use more poetic descriptions of the experiences, emotional states, and characteristic attitudes of the *arahant* authors. This makes sense. If liberation is a radical transformation of perspective, words alone cannot adequately communicate the repercussions of that transformation.

These more poetic descriptions comprise the focus of the rest of this monograph. In this chapter, I am interested only in how the texts use technical terminology. The goal of this chapter is not a philosophical study of the meaning of the technical vocabulary used by the texts to define *nibbāna* (others have done this in far more depth than I)[4] but to compare typical patterns of usage characteristic of each text.

Underlying my analysis is the theory that the authors or redactors of the *Therīgāthā* and *Theragāthā* had access to a pool of stock terms and phrases which was part of the distinctive language of *gāthā* composition (maybe of renunciants in general, as Jain sources contain identical terms and phrases, used in much the same way). In all probability, the verses were composed orally and preserved as part of an oral tradition.[5] They fit easily into the Lord-Parry oral-formulaic theory.[6] Although Lord's work has been criticized for definitional imprecision and problematic assumptions,[7] the insights guiding the theory accord well with my findings. In the theory, the performance of oral epics is inseparable from the composition. Performers string together formulaic phrases, descriptions, and whole passages to construct a tale. They have learned patterns of sounds, rhythms, rhymes and themes by exposure to other performances, and, in their own performances, will choose various combinations and sequences of formulas in the midst of the performance, according to the mood of the audience.[8] In Lord's theory, the formulas a performer employs will evoke other formulas by metrical, stylistic, conceptual, or thematic association. The formulas are thus often linked together, though individual performers will have their own style.[9]

The *Therīgāthā* and *Theragāthā*'s usage of stock terms and phrases appears to follow this theory. The poems use identical vocabulary, follow an identical organizational structure, and often repeat sequences of terms or phrases in identical patterns. Clearly, their authors were members of an established tradition of highly formalized *gāthā* composition. The repetitiveness, structural congruity, and, above all, the use of stock terms and phrases marks this tradition as oral. The fact that both texts use the same formulas indicates that the authors of each share membership in this tradition. But, as I shall demonstrate in this chapter, the texts exhibit subtle variations in their characteristic usage of these otherwise identical stylistic features. The similarity of pattern marks the texts as part of a common tradition; the variance in usage indicates the presence of sub-groups within the tradition.

Liberation Refrains

An initial reading of the texts leaves an impression of similarity rather than difference. The arrangement of the poems in the *Therīgāthā* and *Theragāthā* follows a clear organizational pattern and the poems themselves exhibit structural similarities. Many of the poems in both collections contain both a poetic and a doctrinal section: they begin with a poetic description and end with a recitation of technical terms and phrases which I call a 'liberation refrain'.[10] This pattern is more evident in the longer poems, but even the shorter poems follow it. For example, Meghiya's one-verse poem in the *Theragāthā* begins with a description of the Buddha and ends with Meghiya's attainment of *nibbāna*:

> The great hero, having reached the far shore of all phenomena, counselled me. Hearing his doctrine I dwelt in his presence, mindful. The three knowledges have been obtained, the Buddha's teaching has been done. (*Theragāthā* 66)

Similarly, Aḍḍhakāsī's two-verse poem in the *Therīgāthā* opens with a description of her renounced prostitution, but quickly slips into the stock terminology:

> My wages (of prostitution) were as large as the (revenue of the) country of Kāsī; having fixed that price the townspeople made me priceless in price.
>
> Then I became disgusted with my figure, and being disgusted I was disinterested (in it). May I not run again through the journeying-on from rebirth to rebirth again and again. The three knowledges have been realized. The Buddha's teaching has been done. (*Therīgāthā* 25–26)

Almost all of the poems in both collections follow this pattern, though in a few of the longer poems the stock refrains are interspersed with the more descriptive passages. For example, Soṇa Koḷivisa's poem in the *Theragāthā* opens with his background as a former attendant of a king (632), outlines the doctrinal implications of indolence and mindfulness (633–37), acknowledges the Buddha's instruction (638), and conveys his liberation refrain ('the three knowledges have been obtained, the Buddha's teaching has been done', 639). However, instead of concluding here, as most poems would, this poem continues its doctrinal discussion for another five verses (640–44). This poem, however, is the exception rather than the rule; the majority of poems in both collections that refer to liberation end with a liberation refrain, regardless of the content of the description that precedes it.

In the examples above I have intentionally chosen verses that contain an identical refrain: 'the triple knowledge has been obtained, the Buddha's teaching has been done.' These two phrases are among the fifteen most common stock phrases that make up the liberation refrains in the texts. Appendix A contains a table of the verses that contain these phrases. As translated by K.R. Norman, in the order of their frequency of occurrence in the *Therīgāthā*, they are: desire or craving (*rāga, taṇhā, nicchāta, anupādāya*) overcome; rebirth ended (*amata, macchuhāyin, bhavanetthi samūhata*, etc.); fetters, bonds or sensual pleasures (*yoga, visaṃyutta, kāma, kāmarati*) destroyed;

nibbāna or *nibbuta* (quenched); triple knowledge (*tisso vijjā* or *tevijja*) obtained;[11] freedom (*mutta*, *vimutta*) obtained; *āsavas* (intoxicating ideas, obsessions)[12] destroyed; Buddha's teaching done (*kataṃ buddhassa sāsanaṃ*); pain (*dukkha*, *soka*) gone; darkness torn asunder (*tamokkhandhaṃ padāliya*); peace (*upasanta*, *santi*, *anāvila*) obtained; conquest (*jayati*, *vihanti*, *nihanti*) achieved; rest obtained or the load is put down (*ohito haruko bhāro* or *yogakkhemaṃ anuttaraṃ*); fear (*bherava*, *bhaya*, *dara*) overcome; and, far shore reached (*pāragavesin*).

Each of these phrases appears frequently in the texts, as is readily apparent in Table 1 which documents the total number of occurrences of each term or phrase in each text. The number of occurrences in the *Theragāthā* is naturally higher than those in the *Therīgāthā* as it has almost two and one-half times as many verses (*Theragāthā* 1279; *Therīgāthā* 522). The number in parentheses in the table represents an adjustment for this differential in total number of verses. If the *Theragāthā* contained the same proportion of references to each term as the *Therīgāthā*, its number would correspond to that in the parenthesis.

Contrarily, the numbers are not equivalent between the texts. In particular, the numbers for Knowledge, Freedom, Darkness, Fear, and Far Shore show a significant variation: Knowledge, Freedom, and particularly Darkness are markedly more frequent in the *Therīgāthā*; and Fear and Far Shore are more frequent in the *Theragāthā*.

I will discuss the difference in emphasis underlying this variation in the following section. For now, we should note that these terms and phrases correspond well with the concept of liberation used more generally throughout Pali literature. The term *nibbāna* (quenched) appears very frequently in both texts, as do terms which refer to the doctrinal emphasis on overcoming desire, sensual pleasures, obsessions, pain, fear, and delusion (or ignorance, 'darkness'). The terms of attainment are also well represented: rebirth is ended, the triple knowledge obtained, freedom realized, the Buddha's teaching done, rest achieved, and the far shore reached. In sum, these technical terms imply the process of liberation: the *therīs* and *theras* are liberated from the

TABLE 1

15 Most Common Goal-Referents

Term or Phrase	*Therīgāthā* 522 vss.	*Theragāthā* 1279 vss.
Desire Overcome	33 (83)	87
Rebirth Ended	26 (65)	58
Fetters Cut	25 (63)	57
Nibbāna	23 (58)	58
Knowledge Obtained	20 (50)	35
Freedom	19 (48)	38
Āsavas Destroyed	18 (45)	50
Teaching Done	16 (40)	38
Pain Gone	15 (38)	39
Darkness Torn	14 (35)	3
Peace Obtained	11 (28)	37
Conquest	11 (28)	21
Rest Obtained	5 (13)	17
Fear Overcome	4 (10)	23
Far Shore Reached	2 (5)	19

tendencies that entangle them in the cycle of *saṃsāra*; consequently, they are free of the desires and fears that can be so disturbing, and they can revel in a state of peace and quietude.

Clearly, the texts share a common definition of liberation, or at least, a common vocabulary with which to express it. However, the variation in frequency of occurrence highlighted by the table has significant implications.

Distinctions Between the Texts

The variation in usage of the stock terms or phrases between the texts becomes very prominent when we examine the referents of those terms or phrases. As noted in the Introduction, many of the poems are about rather than by the ascribed author. Other poems are clearly voiced by the *therī* or *thera* to whom the poem is attributed. Yet many poems and liberation refrains are not about the ascribed authors at all. Instead, some refer to individuals known to the ascribed authors while others create hypothetical situations in which any person following the *dhamma* will attain liberation.

I have found that the distinction between refrains that refer to an ascribed author and those that refer to others has an important affect on the texts' tendency to use particular stock phrases. My analysis, therefore, distinguishes between those terms or phrases by or about the ascribed author and those by or about others (named or abstracted)..

In my analysis of the referents of goal-related terminology, I pay close attention to the person to whom attainment is attributed and to verb-tense and verb-referent. The terms I have identified as referring to authors include statements by or about the ascribed author that utilize verbs in the past or present tense and their accompanying gerunds, relative clauses, and adjectival compounds. This 'author' category, therefore, includes statements voiced by a narrator about ascribed authors.

The terms I have identified as referring to others are statements about persons other than the ascribed authors, or statements by or about ascribed authors that incorporate imperatives or future tenses and their accompanying gerunds, relative clauses, and adjectival compounds. This 'other' category, therefore, includes statements by the author about the religious attainments of other individuals, or about the qualities of any individual who has attained the goal. These statements do not refer to the author's own attainments, except, occasionally, as speculations about future accomplishments.

When the narrator or author refers to a future situation, I identify the refrain as 'other'. For example, compare the following excerpts from two poems attributed to Nandā in the *Therīgāthā*. The first fits into my criteria as a reference to 'other', the second to 'author'. In the first, a narrator[13] suggests to her the means by which she can attain the goal and the benefits accruing therein:

> Nandā, see the body, diseased, impure, rotten; develop the mind, intent and well-concentrated, for contemplation of the unpleasant.
>
> And develop the signless, cast out the latent tendency to conceit. Then by the full understanding of conceit, you will wander, stilled (*upasantā*). (*Therīgāthā* 19–20)

This liberation refrain is not about Nandā's attainment of the goal, but rather reflects the narrator's prediction of what her attainment will be like. As a speculation about her future accomplishments, it thus assumes the characteristics of any liberated individual, thereby fitting into the category of 'other'.

The second poem opens with an identical verse voiced by the narrator, but then articulates her answer:

> By (this same) me, vigilant, reflecting in a reasoned manner, this body was seen as it really was, inside and out.
>
> Then I became disgusted with the body, and I was disinterested internally. Vigilant, unfettered (*visamyuttā*), I have become stilled (*upasantā*), quenched (*nibbutā*). (*Therīgāthā* 85–86)

Here Nandā describes the characteristics of her own liberated psyche. The liberation refrain is not about an abstract individual, or even about her own future attainments, but refers directly to her own liberation. This verse I identify as referring to 'author'.

Many of the authors or narrators refer to the attainments of other individuals. For example, Adhimutta's poem in the *Theragāthā* consists of his conversion of a gang of thieves. The thieves are initially impressed by Adhimutta's lack of fear (705–6), so they listen to his recitation of doctrine (707–23). The poem ends with the explanation that while some of the thieves left and did not steal again (724), others joined the *sangha* and attained the goal:

> Having gone forth in the teaching of the well-farer, having developed the constituents of enlightenment and the powers, being clever, with elated minds, happy, with faculties formed, they attained the causally-undetermined state of quenching (*nibbānapadaṃ*). (*Theragāthā* 725)

Similarly, Puṇṇikā's poem in the *Therīgāthā* records her conversion of a *brahman* and concludes with his liberation refrain:

> Formerly I was a kinsman of Brahmā; today I am truly a brahman. I possess the triple knowledge (*tevijjo*), I am endowed with knowledge, and I am versed in sacred lore; (and) I am washed clean. (*Therīgāthā* 251)

Though voiced in the first person, this liberation refrain, like that of Adhimutta's thieves, is not about the ascribed author, but records the successful attainment of an 'other'.

Appendix A contains a detailed table of all references to goal-related terminology, categorized according to this criteria of author-other referents. I have calculated approximate ratios of references to author and other as they reveal significant variations in the texts' usage of technical terminology. My findings are condensed in Table 2. The bracketed numbers under the ratios refer to the actual number of occurrences from which I have calculated the approximate ratios.

TABLE 2

The Author-Other Distinction

Term or Phrase	*Therīgāthā* Author:Other	*Theragāthā* Author:Other
Desire Overcome	3:1 (24:9)	3:4 (40:47)
Rebirth Ended	1:1 (13:13)	4:3 (33:25)
Fetters Cut	5:2 (15:10)	2:3 (23:34)
Nibbāna	3:1 (17:6)	1:5 (10:48)
Knowledge Obtained	2:1 (13:7)	4:1 (28:7)
Freedom Obtained	3:1 (14:5)	1:1 (19:19)
Āsavas Destroyed	3:1 (13:5)	1:1 (24:26)
Teaching Done	4:1 (13:4)	18:1 (36:2)
Pain Gone	1:2 (5:10)	1:8 (4:35)
Darkness Torn	13:1 (13:1)	3:0 (3:0)
Peace Obtained	1:1 (6:5)	2:5 (10:27)
Conquest	11:1 (11:1)	1:3 (5:16)

	Therīgāthā	*Theragāthā*
Term or Phrase	Author:Other	Author:Other
Rest Obtained	1:4 (1:4)	3:2 (10:7)
Fear Overcome	1:3 (1:3)	2:3 (9:14)
Far Shore Reached	0:2 (0:2)	1:8 (2:17)

A glance through Table 2 reveals clear differences in the ways the texts use the language of liberation. Among the most prominent of these differences is the greater frequency of occurrence of the author category in the *Therīgāthā*. Of the seventy-three poems in the *Therīgāthā*, fifty-six, or 76.7 percent, use one or more of these terms to refer to the ascribed author. Only ninety-seven of the two hundred sixty-four poems in the *Theragāthā*, or 36.7 percent, use these terms to refer to their ascribed authors (see Appendix A for the references). Thus, the *Therīgāthā* refers twice as often as the *Theragāthā* to the liberation of its ascribed authors. It is much more 'author-oriented' than the *Theragāthā* – there is a clear tendency to use the language of liberation to refer to its ascribed authors. The main concern of the *Therīgāthā* appears to be the *therīs*' past or present experiences. The text uses liberation refrains with verbs in the past or present tense. In contrast, the *Theragāthā* is less concerned with its ascribed authors and shows a predilection for either references to others or references to the *theras* expressed in imperatives or future tenses. Thus, while both texts use identical terminology, they use it in subtly different ways.

Table 2 also contains interesting differences in the proportions of terms used for authors and others. None of the ratios is identical. The texts exhibit significant variation in their choice of which terms or phrases are appropriate for authors and for others. Many of the ratios are actually reversed. The technical terms Desire (*Therīgāthā* 3:1, *Theragāthā* 3:4), Fetters (*Therīgāthā* 5:2, *Theragāthā* 2:3), *Nibbāna* (*Therīgāthā* 3:1, *Theragāthā* 1:5), and Conquest (*Therīgāthā* 11:1, *Theragāthā* 1:3) are preferred by the *Therīgāthā* for authors, but by the *Theragāthā* for others. Rest is the only term in which the reversal displays an emphasis on authors in the *Theragāthā* against a lack of emphasis in the *Therīgāthā* (*Therīgāthā* 1:4, *Theragāthā* 3:2). I think this difference can be understood with reference to the conceptual underpinnings of the technical language. The terms preferred by the *Therīgāthā* for authors are those that reflect an emphasis on the conquest aspect of liberation. This is perhaps most obvious in the text's marked preference for the term 'conquest' itself, but the other terms used most frequently for authors also reflect this emphasis: desire has to be overcome; fetters have to be cut or otherwise eliminated; *nibbāna* ('quenching') involves the putting out of desires, passions, delusions, etc.; *āsavas* have to be destroyed; and the darkness of ignorance must be 'torn asunder' (*padālita*).

In contrast, the terms used most frequently for authors in the *Theragāthā* convey an emphasis on the attainment aspects of liberation. All the terms showing a significantly higher proportion of authors to others in the *Theragāthā* imply conceptually an end to struggle: rebirth is ended; knowledge is acquired; the Buddha's teaching is completed; and rest is obtained.

When we examine the poems that employ these goal-related terms or phrases, we discover interesting confirmation of this difference in conceptual emphasis. Of the fifty-six poems in the *Therīgāthā* that use the terms or phrases to refer to the ascribed authors, ten describe situations of conflict.[14] Only six of the ninety-seven poems following this criteria in the *Theragāthā* describe conflict.[15]

Of the ten in the *Therīgāthā*, seven appear to represent a stock situation. In each, the poem opens with an adversary questioning various aspects of the *therīs*' religious vocation: Selā is questioned about seclusion (57); Somā about women's intelligence (60); Khemā with sexual temptation (139); Cālā about her disapproval of sectarians (183); Upacālā with sensual pleasures (190); Sīsupacālā with rebirth in one of the heavens (197); and Uppalavaṇṇā with fear of rape (230). Each of these poems is almost identical to those in the *Bhikkhunī Sutta*, though the names of the ascribed authors vary.[16] Each of them also concludes with an identical liberation refrain:

> Everywhere enjoyment of pleasure [*nandi*] is defeated; the mass of darkness (of ignorance) is torn asunder [*tamokkhandho padālito*]; thus know, evil one, you are defeated [*nihato*], death. (*Therīgāthā* 59, 62, 142, 188, 195, 203, 235)

Two of the *Theragāthā*'s poems appear to represent a stock situation similar to that of the *therīs*. Both Vakkali (350–354) and Nhātakamuni (435–440) open their poems with an identical verse voiced by an adversary questioning their ability to withstand harsh conditions in the forest. Their initial response is also identical:

> Brought low by colic, dwelling in the grove, in the wood, where there is a restricted food supply, where it is harsh, how will you fare *bhikkhu*?
>
> Suffusing the body with much joy and happiness, enduring even what is harsh, I shall dwell in the grove. (*Theragāthā* 350–51, 435–36)

From here, their responses differ. Vakkali does not refer to his attainment of liberation, but Nhātakamuni declares himself rid of *āsavas* (439), fetters and pain (440).

The use of these stock situations is quite different in the texts. Where the poems in the *Therīgāthā* vary the questions of the adversary, but employ an identical liberation refrain, those of the *Theragāthā* vary the *theras*' response to an identical confrontation. The presence of the future tense in the *Theragāthā*'s conflict poems also strikes me as significant. Whereas the *therīs* have already attained liberation prior to their confrontation, the *theras* are still seeking the goal, and, indeed, often attain it as a result of the conflict.

In the *Theragāthā* conflict is not generally associated with the experiences of liberated authors. Liberation is presented as an end to struggle; as the completion of the quest. In the *Therīgāthā*, liberated *therīs* continue to experience conflict. Liberation is, in this text, a continuation of struggle; all that has changed is the *therīs*' responses toward it. Though terms used for liberation in both texts are identical, the texts' presentation of liberated authors exhibit subtle differences.

Attitudes towards others also differ between the texts. As we have seen, the *Therīgāthā* is more 'author-oriented' than the *Theragāthā*, but, in a particular way, it is also more 'other-oriented'. The *Therīgāthā* refers quite frequently to the religious attainments of other individuals who have a clear relationship with the *therīs*. Rohiṇī records the liberation of her father after her prolonged explanation of *dhamma* to him (271–290). Cāpā's whole poem is about the accomplishments of her renounced husband who successfully resists her attempts to seduce him (291–311). Sundarī devotes half of her twenty-six verse poem to her father's renunciation and liberation (312–337). Bhaddā Kapilānī (63–66) announces the liberation of her husband, Kassapa. Finally, the poem of Vaḍḍha's Mother (204–212) describes her teaching her son to effectively induce his liberation.

This last example is particularly interesting as the *Theragāthā* contains a poem by Vaḍḍha that corresponds very closely to that of his mother (*Theragāthā* 335–339). Aside from Vaḍḍha, however, references to the religious attainments of other clearly identifiable individuals are relatively infrequent in the *Theragāthā*: Kaṇhadinna expresses happiness at his son's liberation (178); Sarabhaṅga discusses the qualities of the seven Buddhas of past ages (491); Adhimutta records the liberation of the thieves he converts (705); Sela (840) and Ānanda (1021–23) refer to the Buddha's liberation; and Mahāmoggallāna (1168–1169) and Vaṅgīsa (1248, 1249, and 1278) refer to the accomplishments of various *bhikkhus*.

The majority of references to 'others' in the *Theragāthā* are abstract characterizations of a liberated individual. Of the two hundred sixty-four poems in the *Theragāthā*, thirty-nine, or 14.8 percent of all ascribed authors, use the language of liberation to refer to hypothetical, idealized others.[17] For example, Gotama's ten-verse poem is devoted to the lifestyle and characteristics of an ideal ascetic (587–596). It concludes with the liberation refrain of this hypothetical individual:

> A sage should abandon craving [*taṇhā*]; he should split the *āsavas* asunder, root and all; he should dwell released [*vimutta*]; this is fitting for an ascetic.(*Theragāthā* 596)

The *Therīgāthā* contains nothing like this emphasis on such abstract attainments. In fact, Dhammadinnā's one-verse poem is the only reference in the entire *Therīgāthā* that conveys a similar sentiment:

> One should be eager, determinate, and suffused with mind; one whose thought is not attached to sensual pleasures [*kāma*] is called an 'up-streamer'. (*Therīgāthā* 12)

The texts also differ markedly in their characteristic attitudes towards the religious capabilities of others. The *Theragāthā* frequently contrasts the state of unenlightened people with that of liberated individuals. The text is pervaded by references to 'blind, ordinary individuals' (*andhabhūta puthujjana*) who are uncontrolled, impassioned, ignorant fools (*bāla, manda, dummedha*), and are, therefore, inhibited in their ability to hear the *dhamma* clearly or realize its fruits.[18] For example, Yasadatta's whole poem consists of a contrast between fools and the wise:

> Having a hostile mind, the fool hears the conqueror's teaching; he is as far from the true doctrine as the earth is from the sky.
>
> Having a hostile mind, the fool hears the conqueror's teaching; he wanes away from the true doctrine like the moon in the dark fortnight.
>
> Having a hostile mind, the fool hears the conqueror's teaching; he dries up in the true doctrine like a fish in little water.

> Having a hostile mind, the fool hears the conqueror's teaching; he does not thrive in the true doctrine, like a rotten seed in a field.
>
> But he who hears the conqueror's teaching with a joyful mind, having annihilated all his *āsavas*, having realized the state of imperturbability, having attained to highest peace [*santa*], he is quenched [*parinibbāti*], without *āsavas*. (*Theragāthā* 360–364; see also 387–392)

The *Therīgāthā* also refers to fools, though not as frequently as the *Theragāthā*.[19] And the contexts of the *Therīgāthā*'s references differ significantly. Unlike the *Theragāthā* which devotes whole poems to the contrast between the foolish and the wise, all of the *Therīgāthā*'s references are embedded in a context of conversion or confrontation. Puṇṇikā condemns the religious practice of the *brahman* she converts as the teaching of the 'ignorant to the ignorant' (*ajānantassa ajānato, Therīgāthā* 240). Subhā Kammāradhītā refers to fools (*bāla*) who are attracted to sensual pleasures as part of her efforts to convince her relatives to support her renunciation (353). Similarly, Sumedhā's argument with her parents and fiance over her decision to renounce involves her invocation of fools who, bemused by sensual pleasures, will continue on in *saṃsāra* (451–56, 470, 495). Thus, the *Therīgāthā*'s use of the abstract concept 'fool' is very concrete. In order to convince others of the efficacy of the Buddhist path, the *therīs* explain the consequences of the foolish decision not to follow the *dhamma*.

The *Therīgāthā* is consistent in this tendency towards concrete portrayals. As we have seen, the text shows a marked preference for using liberation refrains with reference to its ascribed authors. It also clearly prefers tangible rather than abstract 'others'. And the abstract concept 'fool' is used for very clear purposes. The *Theragāthā* is also consistent, but its tendency is towards abstraction. Almost two-thirds of the liberation refrains in the text refer to others with more frequency than to ascribed authors, and these 'others' are frequently hypothetical, idealized figures rather than named individuals who relate to the *theras*. This is very clear in our analysis of the concept 'fool' in which whole poems, or sections thereof, contrast the perspective of an unliberated individual with that of the 'wise'.

As we will see in more depth in the following chapters, the texts are also consistent in their relative emphasis on conflict. The terms preferred for ascribed authors in the *Therīgāthā* are those that imply conceptually the conquest aspects of liberation while those terms preferred in the *Theragāthā* imply the attainment aspects. The presentation of liberated *therīs* and *theras* confirms this. While the *therīs* who encounter conflict are already liberated, many of the *theras* are still seeking. For the *therīs*, liberation is not an end to conflict, but a continuation. For the *theras*, liberation is an end; conflict is frequently presented as the final event leading up to their liberation experience.

A Difference of Perspective

These differences between the texts' portrayals of liberated authors are very clear when we compare similar poems from the two texts. In the *Therīgāthā*, Subhā Jīvakambavanikā's poem (366–399) presents an extended confrontation between Subhā and a rogue who accosts her in the forest. In the *Theragāthā*, Sundarasamudda (459–465) confronts a courtesan. Both the *therī* and *thera* are tempted with the most attractive elements of the secular world they have renounced, and both successfully overcome this temptation. The poems differ, however, in significant ways that confirm the varying tendencies we have discovered in our previous analyses.

Subhā is on her way to the forest to meditate when a rogue impedes her passage and proposes that she cast off her yellow renunciant's robe and enjoy a sexual interlude with him in the flowering grove (370). Subhā is appalled at his audacity, and instructs him on the essential impermanence of her body: she compares her body to a corpse putrefying in the cemetery (380). Undissuaded, the rogue persists, locating the source of his desire in her beautiful eyes. Subhā attempts again to instruct him, comparing her body to a painted puppet (390) – an inherently composite entity whose animation will delight the eye only as long as its strings are manipulated. Subhā finally resorts to extracting her eye, the source of his desire, and offering it to him (396). Not surprisingly, the rogue's desire ceases abruptly and he begs her forgiveness.

In a recent study, Kevin Trainor aptly describes this poem as a 'kind of literary fugue'[20] in which the contrasting perspectives of Subhā, a liberated *bhikkhunī*, and her obviously unliberated adversary are juxtaposed. While the rogue is enamored with a perception of her body as timelessly beautiful (381), Subhā recognizes the impermanence of her body and the inevitability of its decline. While the rogue understands a worldly life of wealth and comfort as appealing (374–378), Subhā realizes that mundane pleasures are ultimately unsatisfying (386). While the rogue is deluded by the beauty of her eyes, Subhā perceives their true nature as composites of various secretions and fleshly substances (395).

In the poem, the rogue is clearly a personified fool: he is disturbed (*āvilacitta*) and impassioned (*saraja*, 369); he is out of his mind with infatuation (*vimana*, 380); he is confused (*viparīta*, 393); and, following the central metaphor of the poem, he is blind (*andha*, 394). In short, he is the epitome of the 'blind, ordinary individual' (*andhabhūto puthujjana*) referred to in both texts. Subhā's liberated perspective is a clear contrast. Where the rogue's perception (visual and intellectual) is impaired by his passion, Subhā is calm (*anāvila*) and dispassionate (*vītarajam anaṅgaṇaṃ*, 369), her desire has been annihilated (*rāgo hato*, 385), her mind is completely unsoiled (*mano na limpati*, 388), and she is without *āsavas* (389).

Sundarasamudda's poem (459–465) is the only poem in the *Theragāthā* which contains a confrontation similar to that of Subhā. He encounters a courtesan who attempts to seduce him. She is beautiful and offers him wealth and sexual intimacy. Like Subhā's rogue, she refers to his youth. Why renounce now, when he is in his prime? When they are old, they can renounce together, thereby enjoying the fruits of both lifestyles.

Sundarasamudda's courtesan is clearly as much a fool as Subhā's rogue. Like him, she perceives value in transitory sensual pleasures and foolishly dismisses the benefits of renunciation. And, like the other fools in both texts, both the courtesan and the rogue are foils against whom the authors contrast their liberated perspective. The technique of contrast is the same in both texts.

The liberated perspective of the authors is also superficially similar: both are unswayed by their adversary's proposals; both are undistracted by sexual desires; both are immune to the temptation of wealth and worldly power. Like other liberated authors in the texts, they have completely transformed the way they perceive the secular world. Where their adversaries see value, they see peril. They are thus freed from the bonds of *saṃsāra* and have, thereby, attained their goal.

Here, however, the resemblance ends. There are significant differences in the presentation of the liberated authors and their adversaries. The level of character development is not uniform in the two texts. Both the rogue and the courtesan are clearly literary constructs designed to exemplify the temptation renunciants of both sexes must have felt. Neverthless, while Subhā's rogue acquires a clear, if somewhat absurd, personality, Sundarasamudda's courtesan remains a stock character. The poem does not explain her attraction to Sundarasamudda, nor is it concerned with her response to his rejection. In contrast, Subhā's rogue has a clear sexual attraction to Subhā, in particular to her beautiful eyes, and he apologizes profusely when she offers him her eye.

This difference in character development corresponds with the variations we have discovered in our analysis of the referents of goal-related terminology. The rogue's character development complies with the *Therīgāthā*'s tendency towards concrete portrayals of both authors and others. The courtesan's relative lack of character development conforms with the *Theragāthā*'s tendency towards abstraction.

The authors' attitudes towards their adversaries is also consistent with tendencies specific to each text. Like the other *therīs* who refer to fools to convince people about the efficacy of the Buddhist path, Subhā converses with her rogue. She attempts to convert him to her perspective, even resorting to self-mutilation to prove the truth of her contention about the true nature of her body. Apparently her attempt was successful: the rogue recognizes his folly (398).

In contrast, Sundarasamudda does not even reply to the courtesan's proposal. Instead, he simply condemns her:

> When I saw that courtesan beseeching me with cupped hands, ornamented, well-dressed, like a snare of death spread out,
>
> then reasoned thinking arose in me; the peril became clear; disgust with the world was established. (*Theragāthā* 463–4)

This condemnation follows the tendency of the *theras* to present an abstract contrast between fools and the wise. Rather than convert fools to their liberated perspective, the *theras* tend to condemn them.

Subhā and Sundarasamudda also reflect each text's relative emphasis on conflict. Subhā has attained liberation prior to her confrontation with the rogue. She is calm (*anāvila*) and dispassionate (*vītarajam anaṅgaṇaṃ*), and her desire (*rāgo*) and *āsavas* have been destroyed. Sundarasamudda, however, does not attain liberation until after his confrontation. In fact, it is the confrontation that provides the final impetus for his attainment:

> Then my mind was released [*vimucci*]; see the essential rightness of the doctrine. The three knowledges have been obtained [*tisso vijjā anuppattā*], the Buddha's teaching has been done [*kataṃ buddhassa sāsanan*]. (*Theragāthā* 465)

The context of the *therī*'s and *thera*'s liberation experiences confirms the differing emphasis in the texts' characteristic choice of terms for liberation. Where the *Theragāthā* prefers terms that imply completion, and depicts liberated *theras* dwelling in peace and harmony, the *Therīgāthā* tends towards terms that imply conquest, and presents the *therīs* as continuing to struggle, even after they have attained liberation.

Thus, the comparison of these two similar poems highlights the pervasive, if subtle, differences in the texts' use of the language of liberation. My analysis, though, has also underlined the similarities between the texts. The *arahant therīs* and *theras* share a perspective that differs radically from that of ordinary individuals. They simply do not perceive things in the same way as other people, or even as they did prior to their realization of *nibbāna*. The variances we have discovered between the texts must be understood in this light. Though the *therīs* and *theras* use the language in slightly different ways, the differences between them are minor in comparison with the contrast between them and normal folk. Their perspective has indeed been transformed with their experience of liberation.

However, the variations between the texts must also be acknowledged. The similarity of vocabulary, structure, and technique proves only that the authors were members of the same tradition. Their perspective will naturally be shaped by that tradition, particularly when it is expressed in as formalized a medium as these *gāthās*. The fact of consistent difference between the texts is very significant in the context of such obvious formalism. While the texts are clearly designed as companion volumes, directed towards the same purpose (to provide models of success) and organized in an identical manner, the perspective they convey is clearly not uniform. The *therīs* and *theras* express the general worldview of liberated individuals: they understand the pervasiveness of suffering; they accept impermanence; they are immune to the influence of desire, anger, and delusion; and they have attained a state of calm. This does not mean, however, that their perspective is identical.

The authors of both texts are renunciants, but they are also women and men with differing life-experiences who live in segregated communities and who, presumably, recited their verses to sex-specific audiences.[21] The consistent variance in the texts' presentation of the language of liberation could conceivably derive from this very basic difference. As women and men, the authors would probably have been influenced by the gender distinctions of their social world. Their perspective would have been shaped as much from their social context as from their understanding of liberation. In seeking a means of expression to convey their understanding, they would use the vocabulary at hand, but in such a way that conforms with their experiences, and communicates to their audiences.

The perspective of the authors underlies each text's terminology, influences the sequence of formulaic phrases, and dictates the contexts in which liberation refrains are deemed to be appropriate. In the chapters that follow, we will explore some of the repercussions of gender on the ways in which the *therīs* and *theras* perceive other aspects of their lives.

CHAPTER II

Looking Backward: Attitudes Towards Renunciation

> Home have I left, for I have left my world! Child have I left, and all my cherish'd herds! Lust have I left, and Ill-will, too, is gone, And ignorance have I put far from me; Craving and root of Craving overpowered, Cool am I now, knowing *nibbāna*'s peace.
>
> Sanghā, *Therīgāthā* 18[1]

The life of renunciation is intrinsic to the quest for liberation. There are rare occasions in Pali texts in which a person attains liberation prior to renouncing, but, overall, renunciation is viewed as a prerequisite to liberation.[2] Doctrinally, the rationale for this insistence on renunciation is clear: the secular world of family, kinship, occupation, and possessions is seductively attractive. In order to realize the deceptiveness and futility of that attractiveness, women and men must separate themselves from it. It is simply too difficult to 'see things as they really are' while one is immersed in secular life.

The process of attaining liberation itself can be viewed as the successive renunciation of the assumptions, attitudes, and evaluations that characterize the human condition. In attaining liberation, one must disentangle oneself from the emotional, intellectual, and social habits of mind that perpetuate one's continuing existence in the cycle of *saṃsāra*. The first step in this process is the physical act of renunciation. One must initiate the process by transforming one's life-style and behavior. The transformation of one's consciousness follows; first comes the external changes, then the internal.

According to the *Mahāvagga*, shortly after his enlightenment, the Buddha instituted the *bhikkhu-sangha* with the ordination (*upasaṃpadā*) of the five ascetics with whom he had previously performed austerities.[3] Five years later,[4] the *bhikkhunī-sangha* was instituted when the Buddha acceded to his aunt's request for ordination.

In *Cullavagga* X the Buddha is initially very reluctant to open up the *sangha* to women. When his aunt and foster mother, Mahāpajāpatī, requests ordination, the Buddha refuses three times. She and a large number of his female relatives cut their hair, don the yellow robes of renunciation, and follow him to Vesālī. There, standing outside the gate, travel worn, dirty, and miserable, she informs Ānanda, the Buddha's closest attendant, of the Buddha's denial. He takes up her cause and asks the Buddha to ordain her. Again the Buddha refuses three times. It is only after Ānanda changes his approach and asks the Buddha if women could attain *nibbāna* were they allowed entrance into the order that the Buddha changes his mind.[5] He acknowledges their capacity to do so, and concedes the justice of allowing them ordination.

However, conditional to ordination is Mahāpajāpatī's acceptance of eight special rules, the *garudhamma*: *bhikkhunīs* had to pay homage to all *bhikkhus*, even very junior *bhikkhus*; *bhikkhunīs* could not spend the rains independent of *bhikkhus*; *bhikkhunīs* had to ask *bhikkhus* the dates of the *uposatha* rites; *bhikkhunīs* had to confess transgressions before both orders; *bhikkhunīs* must accept discipline from both orders; *bhikkhunīs* had to be ordained by both orders; *bhikkhunīs* could not abuse or revile a *bhikkhu* in any way; and, *bhikkhunīs* could not admonish a *bhikkhu* for any reason. Finally, after accepting women into the order, the Buddha complains to Ānanda that without women, the 'true *dhamma*' (*saddhamma*) would have lasted one thousand years; now that women are in the order, it will last only five hundred years. The eight rules were an attempt to control the damage, like a dike controls a reservoir of water.

There is much scholarly debate about the historicity of this account.[6] However, the date of composition of the story is indisputably early. The story appears in the *Vinayas* of every school of Buddhism extant today, with surprisingly little variation.[7] The Buddha's initial reluctance, his prediction of the decline of the *dhamma*, and the institutional subordination contained in the eight rules are features of the story consistent among all the versions. Clearly, the issue of women's presence in the order was a problem for the community that composed and preserved this story. Even today, in Theravāda countries where the *bhikkhunī-sangha* has died out, the story continues to be cited by those opposed to, and in support of, the reinstitution of *bhikkhunī* ordination.[8]

Furthermore, in accounts of the first council, the quasi-historical gathering of the foremost of the Buddha's disciples shortly after his death, one of the features in common to all extant versions is the reprimanding of Ānanda for his intercession on behalf of women's ordination.[9] The fact that a disciple of his stature is reprimanded at the meeting in which his recitation of the *dhamma* was determined to be canonical is very significant. Though the historicity of this account is also questionable,[10] it does imply that at a very early point in Buddhist history prominent *bhikkhus*, or at least those responsible for keeping the texts, were uncomfortable with women's presence in the *sangha*.

These important texts indicate that the situation in the *sangha* was not egalitarian. *Bhikkhunīs* are explicitly discriminated against, and the Buddha and at least some of the *bhikkhus* were ambivalent about their role in the *sangha*. As many scholars have argued, these features of the *sangha* reflect the gender assumptions of the surrounding social milieu.[11] The social world of ancient India was almost certainly patriarchal. Women were expected to marry, bear children (preferably sons), and serve and obey the men in their families. The lifestyle of renunciation offered women an alternative, but, as we have seen, even in the *sangha*, women were institutionally subordinate to men.

Given this context, it would be surprising if the record of women's religiosity did not exhibit differences from that of men.

When we turn to the *Therīgāthā* and the *Theragāthā*, that is precisely what we find. In this chapter, I will analyze the texts' accounts of the lifestyles of the ascribed authors to discern pervasive patterns of expression that reveal the authors' attitudes towards renunciation. I begin with a study of the texts' presentation of lifestyles prior to renunciation.

The Way They Were

Like many other Buddhist texts, the *Therīgāthā* and *Theragāthā* view renunciation as unquestioningly superior to secular life. As we have seen in the last chapter, those who fail to appreciate the benefits of the monastic lifestyle are unanimously denounced in both texts as 'fools'. Nonetheless, the *therīs* and *theras* also recognize that they themselves were similarly deluded prior to their decision to join the *sangha*, and both discuss their previous values and attitudes with disapproval. The texts thus share a critical stance towards the backgrounds of their ascribed authors.

When we compare accounts of the *therīs*' and *theras*' lifestyles prior to renunciation, however, we find a striking difference. A significantly greater proportion of the *therīs* report situations and conditions of their lives prior to joining the *sangha*. Of the seventy-three poems in the *Therīgāthā*, twenty-five, or 34.2 percent of the ascribed authors provide some kind of history for themselves.[12] In contrast, only twenty-five of the two hundred sixty-four poems in the *Theragāthā*, or 9.5 percent of the ascribed authors provide details of their background.[13] The content of these descriptions also differ: not only do the *therīs* report their previous lifestyles more frequently, but they also provide more detail.

In the *Theragāthā* almost all of the descriptions are oblique or extremely brief. For example, Tissa implies a wealthy background by referring to his renunciation of valuable bowls (97). Similarly, Nanda discusses his previous addiction to ornamentation (157), Jenta Purohitaputta describes himself as 'intoxicated by pride of birth, and by wealth and position' (423), Soṇa

Koḷivisa was 'exalted in the kingdom as the attendant of the king of Aṅga' (632), and Anuruddha alludes to his former wealth and status in his description of being 'attended by song and dance, awakened by cymbals and gongs' (893). Not all of the *theras*, however, lived in such luxurious conditions. Two of Sunīta's twelve verses describe his former poverty (620–21) and Aṅgulimāla discusses his former life of murder and crime, though again with only two verses (880–881).

Some of the *Therīgāthā*'s descriptions of the pre-renunciation circumstances of the *therīs* are also brief and elusive. Sanghā simply informs us that she has given up son, cattle, and what was dear (18); Aḍḍhakāsī implies her former wealth by referring to her large wages as a prostitute (25); Sakulā refers in passing to her abandonment of money and grain (90); Candā describes her poverty as a lack of food and clothing (122); Sujātā alludes to her former wealth by describing her clothing, ornamentation, food, and servants (145–146); and Anopamā describes a suitor willing to pay her father eight times her weight in gold and jewels (153). Other descriptions in the *Therīgāthā*, however, contain much more detail than those of the *Theragāthā*. Four of the five longest poems in the *Therīgāthā*, Sundarī (312–337), Subhā Kammāradhītā (338–365), Isidāsī (400–447), and Sumedhā (448–522), contrast vividly the lifestyles of the *therīs* before and after their renunciation. All of these poems situate their ascribed author in a scenario of complex social interaction. For example, Sundarī's poem consists of a discussion including her father, mother, their charioteer, and an *bhikkhunī* named Vāsiṭṭhī. Sundarī's father is extremely upset over the death of his son and appeals to Vāsiṭṭhī who, prior to her own renunciation, had also mourned excessively. She teaches him about the pervasiveness of suffering, and he decides to renounce thereby initiating the subsequent renunciation of Sundarī and the charioteer. In the course of the discussion, a detailed image of Sundarī's social world is developed: goods are exchanged, people travel between cities, a complex network of relationships is portrayed. The poem presents a bustling scene of secular life that conveys vitality, warmth, and substance.

Isidāsī's poem provides an even more detailed vision of the secular world. Responding to a fellow *bhikkhunī*'s question about what prompted her to renounce, Isidāsī launches into an extended description of her experiences covering several lifetimes. In this life, her father had married her to a rich merchant (406), to whom she offered what she deems to be the best of service: paying obeisance to his parents (407); giving up her seat to his relatives (408); serving food (409); arising before him and approaching him respectfully (410); dressing him as would a servant (411); and cooking and washing for him (412). Despite all this service, her husband rejected her, insisting that she return to her father's house (414). She then married twice more, but was rejected by those husbands as well (421 and 425). She joins the Buddhist *sangha* and quickly attains the triple knowledge (433).

In the *Theragāthā*, there are no comparable descriptions of the *theras*' previous circumstances. The *theras* refer only obliquely and abstractly to their past experiences. The level of abstraction in their accounts evokes a feeling of distance, of detachment towards the secular world. In contrast with the bustling vitality presented in the *Therīgāthā*, the *Theragāthā*'s descriptions are dry and lifeless.

The *Theragāthā*'s accounts are also practically devoid of emotion. Of the twenty-five poems in the *Therīgāthā* that refer to the *therīs*' prior lifestyles, nineteen mention family.[14] Only eleven of the twenty-five poems in the *Theragāthā* recording the *theras*' prior lifestyles mention family.[15] Of these, once again, the *Therīgāthā* contains much more detail.

All of the references to the *theras*' families are cursory. The only situations that even imply a sensitivity to family are Passika who claims his accomplishments will benefit his kin (240–242), Jenta Purohitaputta who condemns his former disrespect for his parents (425), Bhadda who commends his parents for ordaining him at age seven (473–479), and Cūḷapanthaka who records that his brother (apparently a *bhikkhu*) initially turned him away from the gate of a Buddhist *vihāra* (557).

In contrast, the *Therīgāthā* presents the *therīs*' relationships with their family members in great detail and with obvious compassion. Many of the shorter poems contain brief references similar to those of the *Theragāthā* (11, 18, 63, 98, 102, 151, and 163), but the *Therīgāthā* also presents situations that evoke a strong emotional response. For example, even now it is difficult not to sympathize with Kisāgotamī's description of loss and despair:

> Going along, about to bring forth, I saw my husband dead; having given birth on the path, (I had) not yet arrived at my own house.
>
> Two sons dead and a husband dead upon the path for miserable (me); mother and father and brother were burning upon one pyre.
>
> O miserable woman, with family annihilated, immeasurable pain has been suffered by you; and your tears have been shed for many thousands of births.
>
> Then I saw the flesh of my sons eaten in the midst of the cemetery; with my family destroyed, despised by all, with husband dead, I attained the undying. (*Therīgāthā* 215–221)

Even K.R. Norman's stark translation conveys the extreme suffering of Kisāgotamī.[16] Note how Kisāgotamī's experience of *dukkha* relates specifically to her relationships: she mentions the pain of childbirth, but her greatest suffering derives from the death of her family members and the social consequences of her widowhood. Kisāgotamī's experience of social reprobation for losing her family is repeated in Candā's and Vāsiṭṭhī's poems. Candā lacks food and clothing and begs from door to door for seven years because she was a childless widow (122–123). Vāsiṭṭhī, distressed by the death of her son, wanders naked for three years dwelling in rubbish heaps, cemeteries, and highways (133–134).

The *Theragāthā* contains two references to disheartening or distressful circumstances. Cūḷapanthaka is discouraged by his brother's refusal to allow him entrance into the order (557–558) and Sunīta records his unhappy experiences of poverty:

> I was born in a humble family, poor, having little food; my work was lowly — I was a disposer of (withered) flowers.
>
> Despised [or shunned, *jigucchito*] by men, disregarded and reviled, making my mind humble I paid homage to many people. (*Theragāthā* 620–621)

In neither of these examples is the hardship as closely related to the *theras*' social relationships as those described in the *Therīgāthā*. Cūḷapanthaka's grief relates to his frustrated desire to enter the *sangha*, and Sunīta's distress derives from his economic status, not his relationships with family. There is simply no comparison with the extreme grief expressed by Kisāgotamī, nor is there a discussion of the social consequences of family death as described by Kisāgotamī, Candā, and Vāsiṭṭhī. In fact, none of the *theras* report the deaths of family members, nor do they record feeling grief.

However, as we have seen, the *Therīgāthā* reports the grieving of Sundarī's father prior to his renunciation (328). In fact, he is attracted to the *sangha* to alleviate his grief. Similarly, the *Therīgāthā* is markedly more prone to discuss the renounced parenthood of renunciants, both female and male. Of the seventy-three *therīs*, nine refer to their own children,[17] and three more refer to the renounced parenthood of *bhikkhus* they know.[18] Only three of the two hundred sixty-four *theras* refer to children.[19]

This, I think, is closely related to the general disinclination in the *Theragāthā* to discuss the *theras*' previous relationships. This is perhaps most obvious when we examine poems that are almost identical in the two texts. In the *Therīgāthā*, Muttā revels in her freedom by referring to her renounced domestic responsibilities:

> Free am I (*sumuttā*), oh, so free am I (*sādhu mutta*) by being freed (*muttiyā*) by means of the three crooked things: the mortar, pestle, and my crooked husband. (*Therīgāthā* 11; see also 23)[20]

Using identical vocabulary and structure, the *thera* Sumaṅgala glorifies in his freedom from farm labor:

> Free am I (*sumuttiko*), free am I (*sumuttiko*), oh, so free am I (*sāhu sumuttiko*) from the three crooked things: the sickles, the ploughs, and the curved spades. (*Theragāthā* 43)[21]

These poems develop a pun on the word *mutta*, 'freedom,' which refers in each case both to freedom from secular roles and freedom in the religious sense, synonymous with *nibbāna*. The implication is clear: by freeing themselves of their secular roles, Muttā and Sumaṅgala have attained the religious goal, but while Muttā includes her relationship with her husband as one of her secular responsibilities, Sumaṅgala admits no such relationship.

This slight variation in otherwise identical verses confirms the thematic differences we have discovered. The *Therīgāthā*'s descriptions of pre-renunciation experiences revolve around relationships. The secular world the *therīs* renounced is consistently portrayed as a social world in which they were embedded in a network of relationships, especially with family. The *Theragāthā* de-emphasizes the pre-renunciation experiences of the *theras*, and, even in the few descriptions provided, does not dwell at length on the social interactions of the *theras*. Rather, the world the *theras* renounced is portrayed as remarkably asocial.

Breaking Free: Going Forth to the Homeless Life

The implications of this differing emphasis on relationships are two-fold. The *therīs*, enmeshed in a network of relationships, would probably experience more difficulty gaining permission to join the *sangha* than the *theras* who are relatively unencumbered by relationships. Secondly, the *therīs*' close emotional bonds with others could inhibit their ability to attain the psychological detachment required in order to attain *nibbāna*.

If we can accept these accounts at face value, we should also expect conversion to represent a more radical breach for the *therīs* than for the *theras*. The bustling, vital scenes of secular life in the *therīs*' descriptions is in direct opposition to the quiet contemplative atmosphere one would expect of a monastery. The *theras*' reticence in describing the secular world implies a sense of detachment and distance. For them, at least as they are presented in the *Theragāthā*, conversion should represent more of a continuation rather than radical breach.

I think this may help explain the dramatically higher percentage of the *therīs* who discuss the process of conversion. In the *Therīgāthā*, seventeen of seventy-three, or 23.3 percent of all poems, contain references to conversion;[22] only thirteen of two hundred sixty-four, or 4.9 percent of all poems in the *Theragāthā* even mention it.[23] The texts' differing emphasis on relationships is also more pronounced in descriptions of conversion, but in these accounts, the distinguishing feature of the *Therīgāthā* is the frequency and vividness of conflict.

The *Theragāthā* contains only two situations of conflict associated with a *thera*'s desire to go forth. In the first, Ātuma states that he finds it 'hard to go forth because of the wife who has been brought home'(72). His request for permission seems directed at his parents and his relationship with his wife is abstracted; he calls her 'the wife who has been brought home'. In the second, discussed above, Cūḷapanthaka is denied entrance into a *vihāra* by his brother (557). In both cases, the conflict is underplayed. We suspect conflict, but the poems refrain from exploring it in detail.

In contrast, the *Therīgāthā* presents three extended discussions of conflict in the context of conversion (291, 340, and 448). Interestingly, the first, Cāpā's poem, is not so much about her own renunciation but rather portrays her extreme resistance to her husband's decision. Attempting to reverse his decision, Cāpā promises to obey him (295), highlights the beauty of her body (298), and even threatens to kill their son (302). I discuss this poem in greater length below, but for now, we should note that the *Therīgāthā* presents in much greater detail a *bhikkhu*'s conflict with his wife, alluded to only abstractly in the *Theragāthā*.

Sumedhā's poem (448–522), the longest in the *Therīgāthā*, presents a dramatic confrontation between Sumedhā and her parents over her decision to renounce. Sumedhā's parents have arranged a marriage for her with a king and are considerably distraught when she announces her desire to join the *sangha*. Attempting to persuade them to grant her permission to renounce, Sumedhā engages in long discussions of the benefits of renunciation and its fruits (450–459), the transience of material wealth and social position (465–478), and the delusiveness of sensual pleasures (485–513). Her parents and fiance highlight the wealth and social status she will have as a queen (462–464; 483–484). During the conflict, Sumedhā threatens to fast until death (460) and throws herself on the floor (461). Her parents, however, refuse to grant her permission to renounce until her fiance petitions them on her behalf (515) in response to her dramatically throwing her hair on the ground in front of him (514).

Similarly, Subhā Kammāradhītā's poem (338–365) consists almost entirely of her argument with relatives over her decision to renounce, though with none of the high drama of Sumedhā's poem.

The *Theragāthā* contains nothing to compare with these long extended discussions of conflict. Instead, the *Theragāthā* avoids conflict and tends to present the decision as welcome by all concerned.[24] For example, two of the *theras* describe themselves as being given by their parents to the *sangha* when they were only seven years old (473 and 485). Rohiṇī's conversion of her father in the *Therīgāthā* (271–290) is a positive example of a supportive family, but, overall, the relatives of the *therīs* are not overjoyed at their decision to renounce.

A further confirmation of this is the higher proportion of *therīs* who are free of family responsibilities at the time of their conversion. Of the twenty-five *therīs* who provide a background for themselves, eleven are freed: their families are dead or renounced (63, 122, 127, 133, 213, 312); they are very old (102); or, their previous occupation as courtesan (25, 72) or ascetic (87, 107) precluded familial obligations. In contrast, only four of the twenty-five *theras* who record their background are similarly free by means of their great age (108) or prior asceticism (219, 283, 1253). As we shall see in the next section, those *therīs* who are young and beautiful experience the most conflict.

The *Therīgāthā*'s discussions of conversion confirm the high probability of a patriarchal environment in which women must conform with the social roles of wife and mother. The young women who seek to renounce encounter resistance from their families and a large proportion of *therīs* were freed of their social responsibilities prior to joining the *sangha*.

The conversion narratives also confirm the emphasis on relationships we have discovered. The *Therīgāthā* presents a more sociable environment in the context of conversion. Of the *Therīgāthā*'s seventeen references to conversion, eight imply social interaction between a *therī* and other individuals.[25] For example, Puṇṇikā (236–251) and Rohiṇī (271–290) devote their whole poems to their conversion of others; Sundarī's poem (312–337) presents a whole family converting together; Baddhā Kapilānī (63–66) renounces together with her husband, Kassapa; and Sakulā (97–101), Soṇā (102–106), and Candā (122–126) mention approaching a member of the *sangha*. In the *Theragāthā*, there is only a single reference to a *thera* converting others (Adhimutta's conversion of a gang of thieves, 705–725), and only one instance in which a *thera* converts as part of a group (Selā, 818–841).

In place of the *theras* converting others and being converted by members of the *sangha*, the *Theragāthā* stresses the role of the Buddha: eleven of the thirteen *theras* who discuss conversion attribute their conversion to the Buddha.[26] Only five of the seventeen *therīs* who discuss conversion refer to the Buddha.[27] However, in this case, it is the *Therīgāthā*'s references that are more abstract. For example, Anopama's acknowledgement of the Buddha's teachings as the cause of her renunciation is one of the most detailed in the *Therīgāthā*:

> I, having seen the enlightened one, supreme in the world, unsurpassed, having paid homage to his feet, sat down on one side.

> In pity, Gotama taught me the doctrine. Seated on that seat I attained the third fruit.
>
> Then cutting off my hair I went forth into the houseless state... (*Therīgāthā* 154–155)

The *Theragāthā* contains many similarly brief references to the Buddha, but the text also devotes long passages to extolling his greatness. For example, each verse of Selā's twenty-four verse poem praises the virtues of the Buddha (818–841). Selā is overwhelmed by meeting the Buddha, and, along with three hundred *brahmans*, joins the *sangha* as a direct result of his awe. Selā is initially attracted to the Buddha's physical presence:

> You have a perfect body, you are shining, well-proportioned, beautiful to look at; you are golden-coloured, blessed one; you have very white teeth, you are energetic.
>
> For the minor distinguishing marks of a well-proportioned man, all the marks of a great man, are in your body.
>
> You have clear eyes, a round face, you are large, straight, splendid; in the middle of the Order of ascetics you shine like the sun. (*Theragāthā* 818–820)

The Buddha converses with him, informing Selā of the qualities that make him a Buddha, a fully enlightened one (824–831), and Selā encourages his companions to join him in revering him:

> Hear, sirs, what the one with vision says; the dart-remover, the great hero, roars like a lion in the wood.
>
> Having seen him, become Brahmā, unequal led crusher of Māra's army, who would not have faith, even one who is base-born? (*Theragāthā* 832–833)

The *Therīgāthā* contains nothing to compare with this extreme exaltation of the Buddha. Mahāpajāpatī Gotami's poem pays homage to him as the 'best of all creatures' (157), but, overall, the Buddha is a distant, somewhat abstracted figure in the text. In the *Theragāthā*, the Buddha is much more tangible and influential. He is also more human. The

Theragāthā contains references to the physical presence of the Buddha in homey, personable images of his daily life. For example, Soṇa Kuṭikaṇṇa claims to have dwelled with the Buddha and describes him making his bed by laying down his outer robe (365–367). In the *Therīgāthā*, the Buddha is never presented as anything but an object of reverence.

This difference tends to confirm the variations in thematic emphasis we have discovered already. The *therīs* report a much greater proportion of conversions as occurring in the context of social interaction. Conversions by the Buddha are relatively infrequent and tend to lack tangible details. In the *Theragāthā*, the vast majority of conversions occur in the exalted presence of the Buddha and social interaction among *bhikkhus* in the context of conversion tends to be underplayed. I do not think of interactions with the Buddha as particularly social. Even though some *theras* humanize the Buddha more than the *therīs*, he is still an exalted figure.

The presentation of conversion in both texts exhibits both continuity and discontinuity with their descriptions of previous lifestyles. On the one hand, we can view the higher proportion of conversion narratives in the *Therīgāthā* as evidence for the greater significance conversion holds for the text's authors. The detail presented and struggle encountered by the *therīs* tend to confirm this. For the *theras*, conversion is not presented as such a significant event, nor is the contrast between their previous lives and their renounced state as marked as it is for the *therīs*. We could interpret the differing degree of emphasis and contrast as indicating a perception of renunciation as a radical departure from their previous lives for the *therīs*, and as a smooth transition for the *theras*.

The texts also reflect continuity between previous lifestyle and conversion. The *therīs*' presentations of conversion continue the emphasis on relationships we discovered in their accounts of pre-renunciation lifestyles. They may have broken free of the social network in which they were previously enmeshed, but they continue to emphasize the social aspects of their experiences. The *theras*' discussions also reflect continuity, but in their case, their accounts consistently de-emphasize social interaction.

The differing emphasis on past experiences and conversion in the texts implies a differing attitude towards renunciation. The *Theragāthā*'s relative lack of concern with pre-renunciation experiences indicates a conception of renunciation as a complete break with the past. For the *theras*, the circumstances of their lives prior to renouncing do not appear important. The emphasis is on the present. In contrast, the *Therīgāthā*'s readiness to discuss the *therīs*' prior lives conveys a perception of renunciation as transformation rather than breach.

Reflections on the Good Life

When we examine accounts of the *therīs*' and *theras*' experiences in the *sangha*, this difference in emphasis becomes even more pronounced. Of the *Therīgāthā*'s seventy-three poems, eighteen, or 24.7 percent, contain social interactions (conversations, encounters, confrontations, etc.).[28] Of the two hundred sixty-four poems in the *Theragāthā*, only eighteen, or 8 percent, portray similar situations.[29] The figures are nonetheless somewhat misleading. In the *Therīgāthā*, almost all of the poems seven verses or longer record social interactions. When we look at the actual verses devoted to social interaction, we arrive at a figure of 58.2 percent of all verses in the *Therīgāthā*, and only 17.2 percent of all verses in the *Theragāthā*.[30]

Most of the social interactions in the *Therīgāthā* occur in a context of confrontation. The *therīs* frequently encounter adversaries attempting to tempt, frighten, or coerce them into activities inconducive to their chosen lifestyle of asceticism. Selā (57–59), Somā (60–62), Khemā (139–144), Cālā (182–188), Upacālā (189–195), Sīsūpacālā (196–203), and Subhā Jīvakambavanikā (366–399) report such confrontations. Of these, Somā is confronted with doubt of her abilities as a woman to attain the highest goal, Uppalavaṇṇā is confronted with fear of a being woman alone in the forest, Cālā is confronted with doubts about the efficacy of the Buddhist path, and Sīsūpacālā is confronted with the temptation to work towards a divine rebirth. Selā, Khemā, and Subhā Jīvakambavanikā are tempted with the pleasures of sexual intimacy. Significantly, as we shall see below, Selā's and Subhā's adversaries both emphasize the fact that they are alone. In fact, Selā's adversary makes the only reference to a *therī*'s seclusion (*viveka*) in the *Therīgāthā*:

> There is no escape in the world; what will you do by means of seclusion [*vivekena*]? Enjoy the delights of sensual pleasures; do not be a repenter afterwards. (*Therīgāthā* 57)

As we have seen already in the previous chapter (pp. 35–36), Subhā Jīvakambavanikā's poem (366–399) presents the most prolonged and explicitly sexual confrontation in either text. A rogue stops her on her way to the woods. Her response indicates her bewilderment that he should obstruct a *bhikkhunī*:

> What wrong has been done to you by me, that you stand obstructing me? For it is not fitting, sir, that a man should touch a woman who has gone forth. (*Therīgāthā* 367)

He responds that she is young and not ugly and should, therefore, throw away her yellow robe to enjoy the spring with him (370). As part of his temptation, he offers her beautiful clothing, a house, jewelry, a soft bed, and his service if she appeases his desire (372–378). His suggestion that she throw away her yellow robe is particularly revealing. He is not simply asking her to disrobe; rather, he is suggesting that she renege on her vow of celibacy. Furthermore, he attempts to bribe her with the very things she has chosen to renounce: varied clothing, ornamentation, and soft beds.[31]

When we turn to confrontations in the *Theragāthā*, we notice that the *theras* do not report confrontations as frequently or as vividly, nor are the propositions involved the same as in the *Therīgāthā*. Vakkali (350–354), Tekicchakāni (381–386), and Nhātakamuni (435–440) are confronted by an unnamed adversary who questions their abilities to withstand the harsh conditions of outdoor living. Nāgasamāla, Candana, Rājadatta, and Sundarasamudda encounter women and have to confront their desire. Nāgasamāla sees an ornamented dancer on the street (267), Candana sees his wife and child (299), Rājadatta sees a dead woman's body (315), and Sundarasamudda sees and converses with a courtesan (459).

This last example is most significant since it contains the only incident of purposeful temptation found in the *Theragāthā*. All the other temptations derive solely from the *theras*' response to viewing a woman. In Sundarasamudda's poem, the courtesan actually presents an argument as to why he should stay with her and postpone his renunciation:

> You are young to have gone forth. Abide in my teaching; enjoy human sensual pleasures. I (shall) give you wealth; I promise you truly; (if you do not believe me) I shall indeed bring fire.
>
> When we are both old, supported by sticks, we shall both go forth; both ways it will be a winning throw. (*Theragāthā* 461–462)

The courtesan proposes that he can have it both ways: he can enjoy himself now with her, and when they are old, they can both renounce the world and reap the benefits of renunciation. This is the only situation in the whole *Theragāthā* in which a woman consciously tempts a *thera*. The other situations show no such volition on the part of the woman: Rājadatta's 'temptress' is dead and Nāgasamāla's and Candana's are simply standing there. The temptation is found only in the *theras*' minds.

Curiously, the *Therīgāthā* presents a vivid temptation of the *bhikkhu* Kāla by his renounced wife, Cāpā (291–311). Like Subhā Jīvakambavanikā's rogue, she offers him her service (295), but, unlike the rogue, highlights the beauty of her body (297–8), and shows him their son (300). As part of her quest to coerce him back to secular life, she even threatens to kill the child (302). The inclusion of this poem in the *Therīgāthā* strikes me as odd since it is primarily about Kāla, though the commentary points out that Cāpā also renounced and attained liberation soon after Kāla had gone. Even the commentary, though, devotes more attention to Kāla's previous life history than to that of Cāpā.

I think part of the reason for the inclusion of Cāpā's poem in the *Therīgāthā* rather than the *Theragāthā* is the overt conflict contained therein. Subhā Kammāradhītā, Subhā Jīvakambavanikā, Sumedhā, and Cāpā devote most of their lengthy poems to explicit conflict. These poems comprise the longest poems in the *Therīgāthā* and make up one hundred eighty-four of its five hundred twenty-two verses. Though Sundarasamudda's poem in the *Theragāthā* does portray conflict, the collection as a whole contains nothing comparable to the length and detail of these situations in the *Therīgāthā*: Sundarasamudda's poem comprises only seven of the one thousand two hundred seventy-nine verses of the *Theragāthā*.

As we discovered in the last chapter, the *Therīgāthā* displays a consistent conceptual emphasis on conflict. The language of liberation preferred for authors implies the conquest aspects of liberation and a much higher percentage of the liberated *therīs* experience conflict after they have attained liberation. Now we find that a very large proportion of the verses in the *Therīgāthā* are devoted to explicit conflict.

In part at least, the text's emphasis on relationships may help explain this dramatic difference. Conflict is a kind of social interaction. The *Therīgāthā* consistently portrays the characters in the poems engaging in social behavior. The *therīs*' descriptions of their pre-renunciation experiences are filled with conversations and kinship ties. The *therīs* refer relatively frequently to the children they mothered, and report grieving over the deaths of family. They also present men experiencing similar emotions. The *Therīgāthā* refers more frequently than the *Theragāthā* to the parenthood of *bhikkhus*, and it describes a man grieving over the death of his son; a situation never portrayed in the *Theragāthā*. The *Therīgāthā* also presents a confrontation between a *bhikkhu* and his renounced wife that is more detailed and explicit than anything in the *Theragāthā*.

The texts' characteristic emphasis or de-emphasis on relationships continues in descriptions of the *sangha*. The *Therīgāthā* refers frequently to the *therīs* interacting positively with other *bhikkhunīs* in the *sangha*. In the *Therīgāthā*, thirteen of the seventy-three poems, or 17.8 percent, refer to friends or teachers in the *sangha*.[32] In the *Theragāthā*, twenty of the two hundred sixty-four poems, or only 8 percent of the *theras* similarly report friendship.[33]

In the *Therīgāthā*, nine of these references are expressions of gratitude to an instructing *bhikkhunī*: Uttamā (43) and 'A Certain Unknown *Bhikkhunī*' (69) record their instruction by a '*bhikkhunī* who was fit-to-be-trusted;' Paṭācārā (131) and Vijayā (170) report the instruction of a *bhikkhunī*; the 'Thirty *bhikkhunīs*' (119), Candā (124–5), and Uttarā (178) acknowledge Paṭācārā as their instructor; and Subhā Kammāradhītā claims Uppalavaṇṇā as her teacher (363). Perhaps the best example of this gratitude is found in a conversation between Sundarī and the *bhikkhunī* who ordains her:[34]

> 'May that intention of yours, which you seek, prosper, Sundarī. Left-over scraps and gleanings (as food), and a rag from a dust-heap as a robe, these are sufficient. (You will be) without *āsavas* in the next world.'
>
> 'Noble lady, the deva-eye is purified as I undergo training; I know my former habitation, where I lived before.
>
> '(By me) relying on you, o lovely one, o beauty of the Order of *therīs*, the three knowledges have been obtained, the Buddha's teaching has been done.' (*Therīgāthā* 329–331)

Note Sundarī's respect and the instructing *bhikkhunī*'s benevolent disposition. So strong is the affection among the *therīs* that Sumedhā even reports the friendship between herself and two other women that prevailed through thousands of incarnations together (518–19).

In the *Theragāthā*, we find no comparable intimation of long-standing friendship. There are some references to other *theras*' accomplishments (for example, Mahāmoggallāna's homage to Kassapa, the 'heir of the best of the Buddhas' [1109]), but no recognition of fellow *bhikkhu*-instruction. There is one exception, however, in Vaḍḍha's acknowledgement of his mother's instruction (335–39). Significantly, this is also the only reference to a *therī* in the collection.

Instead of the close network of friendships among renunciants present in the *Therīgāthā*, in the *Theragāthā* we find abstract axioms of how *bhikkhus* should associate with 'good companions' and avoid bad.[35] Vimala's poem is representative of the abstraction typical in the *Theragāthā*'s discussion of friendship:

> Avoiding evil friends one should associate with the best of individuals; one should stand fast in his exhortation, seeking the unshakable happiness.
>
> Just as one climbing on to a small plank would sink in the great ocean, so even one who lives a virtuous life sinks if he depends upon an inactive man. Therefore one should avoid that inactive man, who is lacking in energy.
>
> One should dwell with those clever ones who live apart, the noble resolute meditators, (who are) continually putting forth energy. (*Theragāthā* 264–266)

There is no warmth or feeling of human companionship in this or any of the other references to friendship in the text. Instead of the gratitude and mutual concern for the other's welfare evident in Sundarī's exchange with her teacher, we find Vimala comparing a friend to a plank large enough to carry him over the ocean.

Vimala's high regard for those who 'live apart' is also typical of the *Theragāthā*. One of the most striking features of the text is the solitude of the *theras*. They are frequently depicted alone and devote whole poems to the joys of solitude. In fact, references to the theras' solitude outnumber references to the *theras*' social interactions: thirty of the two hundred sixty-four poems, or a full 11.4 percent of the poems in the *Theragāthā* emphasize the *theras*' solitude.[36] Only three of the *Therīgāthā*'s seventy-three poems refer explicitly to the *therī*'s solitude and, in each case, the reference is voiced by an adversary attempting to frighten the *therī*.[37] Where the *theras* often praise solitude and explicitly condemn social interaction, the *therīs* never praise solitude, nor do they have anything negative to say about relationships.

Sabbamitta's poem is perhaps the most explicit condemnation of human interaction in the *Theragāthā*, but the sentiment expressed herein is not infrequent among the references to solitude:

> People are bound to people, people depend on people;
> people are hurt by people, and people hurt people.
> What need then has one of people, or those born of people? Go, leaving this people who have hurt many people. (*Theragāthā* 149–150)

Nowhere in the *Therīgāthā* do we find a condemnation of human interaction per se such as we see in Sabbamitta's poem. This condemnation, I think, is very revealing. The *theras*' tendency to neglect social interaction is not simply an oversight on their part. The *theras* are too consistent in their attitudes towards relationships: they praise solitude, condemn human society, and refrain from presenting even positive interactions among the *theras*. These features of the text imply a clear perception of renunciation as complete separation from society. Emotional bonds with others, even those beneficial to the quest for liberation are simply not part of the *theras*' vision of renunciation.

In contrast, the *therīs*' continuing emphasis on relationships implies a differing perception of renunciation. Close attachments with others are fraught with difficulty and can produce emotions such as fear, grief, and desire that are antithetical to liberation. Yet, in the *Therīgāthā*, relationships can also prove beneficial to the quest for liberation. For the *therīs*, renunciation does not mean the complete severing of relationships but their transformation. Instead of entangling the *therīs* further in the bonds of *saṃsāra*, the *therīs*' relationships in the *sangha* assist them in releasing the bonds.

The *therīs* also work hard to help others. They not only relate positively to other *bhikkhunīs*, but they actively engage in attempts to convert others to their liberated perspective. The *theras* also occasionally converse with others outside the *sangha*, but they tend more frequently to condemn rather than convert.

We see, therefore, that the 'good life' looks very different from the perspective of each text. In the *Therīgāthā*, the *sangha* is very social. It is embedded in a social context, and the *therīs* interact frequently with other *bhikkhunīs*. In the *Theragāthā*, the *sangha* is not so social. The *theras* appear to spend much of their time alone, and they do not present many interactions among themselves. This perspective has important implications for the self-image of the *therīs* and *theras*. If, as seems probable, one's social context influences one's worldview, and particularly one's formal, public expression of that worldview, we should expect to find the impact of such a dramatically differing emphasis on social discourse in the ways the *therīs* and *theras* perceive themselves.

CHAPTER III

Looking Inward: Attitudes Towards the Body

> Behold, Nandā, the foul compound, diseased, Impure! Compel thy heart to contemplate What is not fair to view. So steel thyself And concentrate the well-composed mind. As with this body, so with thine; as with Thy beauty, So with this–thus shall it be With this malodorous, offensive shape. Wherein the foolish only take delight. So look thou on it day and night with mind Unfalteringly steadfast, till alone, By thine own wit, delivered from the thrall Of beauty, thou dost gain vision serene.
>
> Sundarī-Nandā, *Therīgāthā*, 82–84[1]

The human body has posed problems for all religions of the world. All religions have something to say about the body, whether to regulate its natural processes through rules of purity and defilement; to condemn or celebrate its biological capacities for illness, disability, or regeneration; to control or glorify its procreative functions; to ritualize its passages through stages of growth. The response in Pali texts to the problem of the body is to attempt to transform our psychological attachment to it into an analytical detachment.

The body is a particularly strong source of sensations ranging from pleasure to pain, desire to disgust. It provides the basis for our sense of self and continually imposes pressures upon our intellect and emotions for fulfillment of its biological needs. As such, the body poses a powerful obstacle for those seeking the Buddhist goal of liberation from all ties, from a delusory perception of permanence and stability, and, above all, from a false conception of self as real and abiding in any tangible sense.

The issue of Buddhist attitudes towards the body has been one of the most contentious among scholars who have studied the role and image of women in Buddhism. The vast majority of Pali texts were written by celibate men and reflect their perceptions of women's bodies as enticing obstacles to their quest for liberation. Many of these perceptions reveal a misogynist distrust, fear, and antagonism towards the female body.

In my opinion, the most problematic issue under the rubric of Buddhist attitudes towards the body is the fact that depictions of all bodies and bodily processes are not uniform: women's bodies are more frequently described as impure and defiling than are men's bodies; women are often presented as inherently more physical, that is, as tied more closely to bodily processes than are men; and, concomitantly, women are commonly defined by their sexuality and are presented in some texts as insatiably lustful.

In her work *Women in Buddhism*, Diana Paul outlines this portrayal of women as purely sensual, explaining that non-Buddhist Indian texts portray women's sexual drives as stronger than men's. In the Buddhist adaptation of this belief,

> woman glowed with a much more intense sexual vitality and was the primeval force of fecundity, as she was in the Hindu religion. Unlike the Hindu Mother Goddess, however, the sexual energy was unequivocally repugnant in early Buddhist sects such as the Theravādin sect. What was feminine or sensual was *saṃsāra*, the world of bondage, suffering, and desire, which led to cycles of rebirths.[2]

Nancy Falk picks up the same theme more forcefully than Paul, contending,

> a woman was a veritable image of becoming and of all the forces of blind growth and productivity which Buddhism

> knew as *saṃsāra*. As such she too was the enemy – not only on a personal level, as an individual source of temptation, but also on a cosmic level, as representation and summation of the processes binding all men. And she especially had to be over-come, if liberation was to remain a possibility.[3]

There are many passages and incidents throughout the Pali canon to support this view of Buddhist misogyny. For example, the Buddha's prediction that women's entrance into the *sangha* would halve the lifetime of true *dhamma* indicates a perception of women as dangerous. The similes used by the Buddha to describe the harmful effect of women's presence illustrate the contaminating nature of women: the Buddha compares the *sangha* with women in it to a house prey to robbers, a ricefield struck by mildew and a sugar cane field attacked by red rust, stipulating that he had attempted to control the threat of feminine contamination by the 'great reservoir' of the eight rules for *bhikkhunīs*.[4]

Clearly in this text, women represent an extremely powerful metaphysical threat to the *dhamma*. As many scholars have noted, *dhamma* is one of the central religious concepts in Theravāda Buddhism.[5] It refers not only to the Buddha's teachings, but also to the means by which individuals follow those teachings and the Truth those teachings convey. If women's presence is as contaminating as these similes indicate, the threat to the *dhamma* they pose is insidious, contagious, and devastating.

The first of the four *Pārājika* offenses, sexual intercourse, for which expulsion from the *sangha* is mandatory, echoes this portrayal of women as dangerously defiling and contaminating. In the account of the first infraction, the Buddha rebukes the offender stating:

> It were better for you, foolish man, that your male organ should enter the mouth of a terrible and poisonous snake, than that it should enter a woman. It were better for you, foolish man, that your male organ should enter the mouth

of a black snake, than that it should enter a woman. It were better for you, foolish man, that your male organ should enter a charcoal pit, burning, ablaze, afire, than that it should enter a woman.[6]

The Buddha then explains that sexual intercourse has led the offender into what is 'not verily *dhamma*, upon village *dhamma*, upon a low *dhamma*'. Here the threat predicted in *Cullavaga X* is developed further. Not only do women threaten the *dhamma* by their presence in the *sangha*, but sexual contact with a woman causes a man to enter into what is not *dhamma* (*asaddhamma*).

The issue here is not simply the violation of a code of conduct. None of the other *Pārājika* offenses involves the offender's entrance into false *dhamma* or uses snake imagery to symbolize the danger of prohibited activities. Furthermore, in the account of the first instance of a *bhikkhunī* breaking the first *Pārājika* rule, there is no mention of her entering into what is not *dhamma* as a result of sexual contact with a man.[7] Rather, the danger of metaphysical contamination is reserved for men who engage in sexual contact with a woman. Apparently this contact has devastating effects. The *bhikkhu* who first transgressed the rule became ill and began to waste away.[8]

These examples highlight the perception of women as dangerous to celibate *bhikkhus* and suggests that women's sexuality is the source of this danger. Other passages in the canon explicitly describe women as insatiably lustful. For example, the *Aṅguttara Nikāya* has the Buddha saying:

> Monks, womenfolk end their life unsated and unreplete with two things. What two? Sexual intercourse and childbirth. These are the two things.[9]

In the same collection, we find the behavioral consequences of this inherent nature:

> Monks, a woman, even when going along, will stop to ensnare the heart of a man; whether standing, sitting or

lying down, laughing, talking or singing, weeping, stricken, or dying, a woman will stop to ensnare the heart of a man. Monks, if ever one would rightly say: 'It is wholly a snare of Māra, verily, speaking rightly, one may say of womanhood: It is wholly a snare of Māra.'[10]

Thus we see a tendency in Pali texts to describe women as contagiously impure, powerfully dangerous, and inherently lascivious. This is not the only kind of presentation of women in Pali texts,[11] but the tendency to present women this way is clear and appears to be very strong. The perspective, however, is clearly that of celibate *bhikkhus* who struggle against their own sexual desires. The image above of a woman on her deathbed seeking to seduce a man illustrates the ludicrous extent to which sexual repression is directed outward.

In this chapter, I am interested in discovering the perspective of the *therīs* and *theras* towards the body. If the tendency towards a misogynist distrust and fear of female sexuality was, in fact, current in the *sangha* at the time of composition of our texts, how did it affect women's self-image? Do the *therīs* and *theras* appear to feel the same way about their bodies? How do they respond to sexual desire? These are the questions guiding my analysis in this chapter.

A Buddhist Lesson in Anatomy

The *Therīgāthā* and *Theragāthā* share a general Buddhist view of the body as an impermanent composite of various elements. Human attractiveness is delusory, the product of our desires and misleading tendencies to seek fulfillment in something that is ultimately insubstantial. Rather than seeing the body as attractive and desirable, the texts counsel a view of the body 'as it really is', as a collection of various organs, membranes, and fluids, enclosed within a deceptively appealing outer covering. In Buddhist texts, a decomposing corpse is a more accurate vision of the true nature of the body than is the romantic vision of physical perfection.

The vision of physical perfection is nonetheless very strong. Our notions of physical attractiveness may be influenced by cultural definitions of beauty, but the source of those attractions is human sexuality. Buddhism designed drastic measures to combat this strength, perhaps the most effective and dramatic of which is the corpse meditation. Buddhist practitioners are urged to meditate on decomposing corpses to understand the transiency and composite nature of the body. Practitioners are then urged to consider how their own bodies are similarly composed.[12]

This meditation should result in an analytical detachment towards all human bodies by its vivid illustration of the true nature of the body. Every time those who have meditated in this manner feel physical attraction to a particular body, they should be reminded of the oozing putrefaction contained therein. Rather than the beautiful, timeless entity in romantic notions of beauty, they should envision the body as a composition of bones, flesh, blood, and skin. The corpse meditation reveals in dramatic and emotionally powerful images that there is no essential quality of the body–nothing fixed, enduring, or truly substantial.

The *Therīgāthā* and *Theragāthā* appear to share the perspective encouraged by the doctrinal emphasis on bodily decomposition. Both texts contain meditations on decomposing corpses, whether real or simply imagined. These descriptions are very similar. They unanimously convey an attitude of disgust and disapproval for the body and its functions, but when we look closely at these descriptions, we discover that female and male bodies are not portrayed in the same way. None of the descriptions of post-mortem decay, bodily secretions, or internal substances refers explicitly to male bodies or bodily functions. Additionally, with only one exception (Kappa, *Theragāthā*, 567), those bodies that are of an unspecified sex are designated female by the commentary.

Looking first at the *Therīgāthā*, we find six descriptions of bodily putrefaction, three of which are addressed to the *therī*: Abhayamātā is urged (by her son, according to the commentary), 'Mother, upwards from the sole(s) of the feet, downwards from the head and hair, consider this impure, evil-smelling body' (33); and both Nandās are advised to 'see the body, diseased, impure, rotten' (19 and 82). The remaining three all occur in contexts of conflict. In response to the adversary attempting to seduce her, Khemā claims to be 'afflicted by and ashamed of this foul body, diseased, perishable' (140). Similarly, Sumedhā asks her parents:

> Why should I cling to this foul body, impure, smelling of urine, a frightful water-bag of corpses, always flowing, full of impure things?
>
> What (do) I know it to be like? A body is repulsive, smeared with flesh and blood, food for worms, vultures, and (other) birds. Why is it given (to us)? (*Therīgāthā* 466–467)

Finally, Subhā Jīvakambavanikā informs her adversary that her body is 'full of corpses, filling the cemetery, of a breaking nature' (380).

Dhammapāla designates the Buddha as the speaker in both Nandās' poems, explaining that he had conjured up an image of a beautiful woman growing old and decrepit because both *therīs* were infatuated with their own beauty.[13] Though the commentary is not always the best guide to interpretation, in this case, it is consistent with both texts in associating impurity and disease with female bodies.

The *theras* echo this use of the female body in descriptions of bodily impurity. The *Theragāthā* contains seven references to impurity and decomposition. Of those, five refer explicitly to women's bodies: Rājadatta (315) and Kulla (393) see a woman's corpse; Sabbakāma contemplates a woman's form, using imagery of post-mortem decay (453); Pārāpariya repeats this imagery, adding that the body is full of pus (736–739); and Mahāmoggallāna directs a particularly vituperative monologue against a woman which graphically illustrates his disgust for her body:

> You little hut made of a chain of bones, sewn together with flesh and sinew. Fie upon the evil-smelling body. You cherish those who have another's limbs.
>
> You bag of dung, tied up with skin, you demoness with lumps on your breast. There are nine streams in your body which flow all the time.
>
> Your body with its nine streams makes an evil smell and is obstructed by dung. A *bhikkhu* desiring purity avoids it as one avoids excrement. (*Theragāthā* 1150–1152)

Significantly, the commentary designates the recipient of this speech as Vimalā, the *Therīgāthā*'s former courtesan (*Therīgāthā* 72–76), who allegedly attempted to seduce Mahāmoggallāna.[14] Similarly, the commentary has Nandaka directing his 'curse upon bodies, evil-smelling, on Māra's side, oozing' (279) to his former wife.[15]

In each of these instances the *thera* contrasts the fools who are attracted to such a body with the liberated perspective of those who are not.[16] Pārāpariya's poem explains how a woman's form can easily deceive a man who has not attained the perspective of liberation:

> (The body) full of pus, and blood, and many a corpse, is made like a beautiful painted box by skilful men.
>
> One is not aware that that which has a sweet taste is bitter, that the bond with those who are dear is painful, like a razor smeared up and down with honey.
>
> Passionately attached to the form of woman, the sound of woman, and the touch of woman too, (and) the scents of woman, one finds various sorts of pain. (*Theragāthā* 736–738)

The consequences of failing to see the body 'as it really is' are serious. Frequently, the *theras* predict death and entrapment to those who value the body. A woman's physical form is compared with a hunter's snare, into which an 'ordinary individual' is lured.[17] Once caught, the individual is bound to experience death and continued rebirth and redeath:

> As luring deer with a snare, as fish with a hook, as a monkey with pitch, so they trap an ordinary individual.
>
> (Namely) pleasant sights, sounds, tastes, smells, and things to touch; these five strands of sensual pleasure are seen in a woman's form.
>
> Those ordinary individuals who with impassioned minds pursue them (i.e. women), fill up the terrible cemetery. They heap up renewed existence.
>
> But he who avoids them as one avoids a snakes's head with one's foot, he being mindful overcomes this attachment to the world. (*Theragāthā* 454–457)

Clearly, attraction to a woman's body is fraught with danger.

There is, however, one poem in the *Theragāthā* in which the sex of the offensive body is unspecified either by the author or commentator. Kappa's whole poem is devoted to a contemplation of the body as foul, oozing, delusory and reminiscent of excrement (567–576). The use of identical imagery to the previous examples, however, indicates common themes between this poem and others focussing specifically on female bodies: the body is described as 'full of pus', oozing foully (568) and as composed of a 'binding of sixty tendons, plastered with fleshy plaster, girt with a jacket of skin' (569). Finally, Kappa concludes:

> The blind ordinary individuals who cherish this body fill up the terrible cemetery; they take on renewed existence.
>
> Those who avoid this body like a dung-smeared snake, having spurned the root of existence, will be quenched without *āsavas*. (*Theragāthā* 575–576)

The use of identical imagery to those poems referring to women's bodies may reflect only a common perception of all human bodies, but Kappa's conclusion is too similar to another conclusion to be considered truly generic. Sabbakāma's depiction of a woman's form as an 'impure, evil-smelling (body), full of various corpses, oozing here and there, (that) is cherished' (453) recalls Kappa's individuals who cherish the body. Likewise Sabbakāma also concludes that those foolish enough to do so will 'fill up the terrible cemetery' (456), 'but he who avoids them as one avoids a snake's head' overcomes attachment to the world (457). In both cases, attraction leads inevitably to death, just as close contact with a poisonous snake would. These similarities give us good reasons for suspecting that Kappa's object of meditation is female.

If we accept this analysis, we see that all the disgusting bodies contemplated by the *theras* are female. The imagery is consistent in associating women's bodies with impurity, contamination, and death. Like the first *Pārājika* offence, in which sexual contact with a woman is equated with sexual contact with a poisonous snake, these examples use snake imagery to illustrate the danger of attraction to a woman. And, like the contamination women bring to the *sangha* in the similes of disease and devastation predicted in *Cullavagga X*, those who do not avoid women face death and destruction.

Turning back to the *Therīgāthā*'s descriptions of the decomposing bodies, we discover some interesting points of comparison. The *therīs* also concentrate on women's bodies as evil-smelling, impure, containing corpses, and oozing. However, none of the *therīs* employ snake-imagery, nor do they predict the demise of those foolish enough to be attracted to them. In fact, the *therīs* tend to use cemetery imagery to refer to their own bodies rather than to predict the fate of fools deluded by bodily attractiveness.

For example, Subhā Jīvakambavanikā instructs her adversary about the falseness of his desire, reminding him that her body is eventually bound for a cemetery (380). Similarly, Sumedhā informs her parents of the true nature of her body:

> The body is soon carried out to the cemetery, devoid of consciousness; it is thrown away like a log by disgusted relatives.
>
> Having thrown it away in the cemetery as food for others, one's own mother and father wash themselves, disgusted; how much more do common people?

> They are attached to the unsubstantial body, an aggregate of bones and sinews, to the foul body, full of saliva, tears, excrement, and urine.
>
> If anyone, dissecting it, were to make the inside outside, even one's own mother, being unable to bear the smell of it, would be disgusted. (*Therīgāthā* 468–471)

The imagery here is identical with that found in the *Theragāthā*, but, instead of predicting the cemetery for those who are attracted to such a body, the *therīs* predict the cemetery for themselves. They refer to the cemetery to instruct others about the true nature of their own bodies, not to illustrate the ways in which attraction to human bodies leads to death.

The *therīs* thus personalize the Buddhist lesson in anatomy. The vision of a putrefying corpse is internalized; it is their own bodies that are filled with disgusting substances and their own bodies that will fill the cemeteries. The *theras* abstract this lesson. The disgusting nature of the body is revealed not in images of self, but in images of others, particularly women. It is not their own bodies that will fill the cemeteries, but the bodies of those fools who feel attraction for the female form. However in both texts, the body poses a problem. Both *therīs* and *theras* must come to understand the true nature of the body and both must overcome an attraction to it.

The Body Beautiful

While both texts share a vision of the true nature of the body as a putrefying corpse, both also acknowledge the power of physical attraction. In the Buddhist worldview, beauty is not an inherent property of a given object, but rather, is the product of human artifice. Ordinary individuals are enthralled by their own desires and fail to see through the deception. Liberation involves the elimination of those desires and the deluding filter they impose upon perception. The *Therīgāthā* and *Theragāthā* combat the delusory attractiveness of the body with descriptions of the artificial nature of beauty.

The *Therīgāthā* contains two poems describing the artifice required of women to make themselves beautiful (72–76 and 366–399). In the first, Vimalā describes herself as a prostitute prior to renunciation:

> Intoxicated by my (good) complexion, my figure, beauty, and fame, haughty because of my youth, I despised other women.
>
> Having decorated this body, very variegated, deceiving fools, I stood at the brothel door, like a hunter having spread out a snare, showing my ornamentation. Many a secret (place) was revealed. I did various sorts of conjuring, laughing at many people. (*Therīgāthā* 72–74)

She is fully aware that her attractiveness is a human construction. She is also aware of the dangers her body poses to those foolish enough to desire it: she compares her body to the snare of a hunter.

As we have seen in our analysis of the corpse imagery above, the *Theragāthā* frequently describes the fatal consequences of attraction to the female body. In the text's discussions of the artificial nature of beauty, the lethal overtones of the hunter's snare found in Vimalā's poem are developed further. Six of the *theras* describe women's bodies as a snare of death. Nāgasamāla encounters a dancing girl, 'ornamented, well-dressed, like a snare of death spread out' (268). Candana and Sundarasamudda employ identical imagery, Candana for his renounced wife (299), and Sundarasamudda for a courtesan (463). Nandaka (281), Sabbakāma (454), and Raṭṭhapāla (774–5) all use the same imagery, but in the abstract. They do not identify the source of their contemplation, but simply curse the artificial beauty of women's bodies as a snare. For example, Raṭṭhapāla presents an extended discussion of the deceptive artifice underlying feminine beauty:

> See the painted puppet, a heap of sores, a compounded body, diseased, with many (bad) intentions, for which there is no permanent stability.

> See the painted form, with jewels and ear-rings; covered with skin and bones, it is resplendent with clothes.
>
> The feet are reddened with lac, the face is smeared with powder, enough to delude a fool, but not for one who seeks the far shore.
>
> Hair braided eight-fold, eyes smeared with collyrium, enough to delude a fool, but not for one who seeks the far shore.
>
> The ornamented foul body is like a new painted collyrium box, enough to delude a fool, but not for one who seeks the far shore.
>
> The hunter laid his net; the deer did not come near the snare; having eaten the fodder, let us go while the deer-trapper laments. (*Theragāthā* 769–774)

Both texts use the same imagery of the hunter's snare to describe the deceptive beauty of a woman's body. However, as Karen Lang has discovered in her study of this imagery, the descriptions of a hunter laying a trap are used differently in the two texts. Where the *therīs* recognize 'themselves as the hunters, men the prey, and their bodies as the baited snare,'[18] the *theras* see Māra as the hunter, 'men as the hunted prey, and women's bodies as the baited snare.'[19] Where the *therīs* identify closely with Māra, and the realm of ceaseless reproduction and suffering he represents, the *theras* objectify the threat, attributing it not to themselves but to women. Where the *theras* use snare imagery to describe the fatally deceptive attractiveness of other's bodies, Vimalā uses it to describe her own.

But both texts use this imagery to refer to women's bodies. In neither text is there any reference to a male body as a deceptively attractive snare. There is, however, one example of an attractive man in the *Therīgāthā*. Like the women in the *Theragāthā*, Sumedhā's suitor is handsome (462), and, like them, he is adorned in gold and jewelry as he beseeches her to marry him (482). In contrast with the *theras*' perception of the lethal trap contained in women's bodies adorned in this way,

Sumedhā sees the folly of relying upon one who is ultimately impermanent:

> What will another do for me when his own head is burning? When old age and death are following closely one must strive for their destruction. (*Therīgāthā* 493)

Rather than condemn her suitor for his deceptive beauty, and revel in her own escape from the potential trap of desiring his body, Sumedhā uses the imagery to instruct her parents about the inevitability of physical decline. She does not refer to a hunter's snare, nor does she predict the demise of those foolish enough to be entrapped by desire. Instead, she discusses the impermanence of all people and all things. Her presentation of masculine attractiveness, therefore, does not emphasize the deceptiveness and lethal qualities of that attractiveness, but rather, the essential transience of all things.

Thus, while both texts disapprove of physical attraction and while both discuss the artificial nature of beauty, the texts differ in the degree of self-identification portrayed by the ascribed authors. While Vimalā describes the artifice she employed to attract men and Sumedhā extrapolates the inevitable decline of her suitor's beauty to all things, including herself, the *theras* neither describe their own enhancement of physical attractiveness, nor do they recognize that the female bodies they condemn are in any way similar to themselves.

This becomes even more clear when we compare the texts' presentation of the image of a painted puppet. The *Theragāthā* contains three identical verses describing the painted puppet:

> See the painted puppet, a heap of sores, a compounded body, diseased, with many (bad) intentions, for which there is no permanent stability. (*Theragāthā* 769, 1020, 1157)

The painted puppet poses a triple danger: it is diseased, malicious, and impermanent. Close contact with it could result in contamination, defilement, and disillusionment. If, overcome with desire for it, one tries to grasp the puppet, one soon discovers its composite and delusory nature. The attractive covering of the puppet only exacerbates its danger. Like deceptively attractive women, the lethal danger of the puppet is concealed. And, like the beauty of women, the puppet is made attractive by human hands, designed to engage the audience in a pleasurable fantasy.

As in the other examples of the deceptiveness of human beauty, however, the texts differ in the way they use this imagery. The *Therīgāthā* contains only one reference to a painted puppet. As part of Subhā Jīvakambavanikā's attempt to instruct her adversary of the futility of his desire for her, she resorts to the imagery of the painted puppet:

> ... well-painted puppets, or dolls, have been seen by me, fastened by strings and sticks, made to dance in various ways.
>
> These strings and sticks having been removed, thrown away, mutilated, scattered, not to be found, broken into pieces, on what there would one fix the mind?
>
> This little body, being of such a kind, does not exist without these phenomena; as it does not exist without phenomena, on what there would one fix one's mind?
>
> Just as you have seen a picture made on a wall, smeared with yellow orpiment; on that your gaze (has been) confused; (so) the wisdom of men is useless.
>
> O blind one, you run after an empty thing, like an illusion placed in front of you, like a golden tree at the end of a dream, like a puppet-show in the midst of the people. (*Therīgāthā* 390–394)

Once again, the *Therīgāthā* employs the imagery to refer to the *therī*'s own body.

None of the *theras* describes themselves in this way. According to the commentary, Ānanda's verse is directed to either Uttarā, a *bhikkhunī* enthralled by her own beauty, or to those men who were infatuated with Ambapālī, a renowned courtesan.[20] Raṭṭhapāla's reference to the painted puppet is part of his contemplation of a heavily ornamented woman (770–74). He describes her ornamentation in detail, focussing on her jewels and ear-rings (770), her foot and face paint (771), and her elaborately braided hair (772). His contemplation culminates in an allusion to the hunter imagery: 'the hunter laid his net; the deer did not come near the snare' (774). Similarly, Mahāmoggallāna's use of the puppet imagery concludes his vehement condemnation of a woman as evil-smelling, flowing foully, and comparable to excrement (1150–1156).

Subhā's reference to the painted puppet also differs from those of the *theras* in her use of it to instruct her adversary. Rather than simply condemning the object of contemplation for being a 'painted puppet', the *therīs* use the imagery to convert others to their liberated perspective. Apparently, Subhā's instruction was effective. After she gives her adversary her eye, the source of his desire, his passion ceases abruptly and he begs her forgiveness: 'Having smitten such a person, having as it were embraced a blazing fire, I have seized a poisonous snake' (398).

This concluding statement is quite puzzling. Subhā has done nothing threatening to the rogue other than to show him the error of his ways by reciting basic doctrine. Why then does he refer to her as a poisonous snake? In light of the analysis of snake imagery above, we might speculate that Subhā's lectures were effective in instilling in him the notion of the dangerous impurity and deceptiveness of the female body. He uses the same imagery as the *theras* when describing a dangerously close encounter with a woman. This is the only case in the *Therīgāthā* of a reference to snake imagery in conjunction with a description of the body. Significantly, the text has a man voicing it in reference to a woman's body.

This example highlights a contrast between the texts' attitudes towards the body that pervades all the examples cited thus far. While the *therīs* personalize images of the body as impure, *theras* objectify them and project them onto others, namely women. This is graphically illustrated in a conversation in the *Theragāthā* between Vaṅgīsa and the Buddha. Vaṅgīsa complains of burning with desire for sensual pleasures. The

Buddha's advice can be seen as an invitation for him to project his desires outward:

> Your mind is on fire because of perversion of perception. Avoid pleasant outward appearance, accompanied by desire.
>
> See the constituent elements as other, as pain, not as self; quench the great desire, do not burn again and again.
>
> Devote the mind, intent and well-concentrated, to contemplation of the unpleasant. Let your mindfulness be concerned with the body... (*Theragāthā* 1224–1225)

His instruction for Vaṅgīsa to 'devote his mind, intent and well-concentrated, to contemplation of the unpleasant' (*asubhāya cittaṃ bhāvehi ekaggaṃ susamāhitaṃ*) is one of the few phrases that is repeated identically in the *Therīgāthā* in the poems attributed to Nandā (19 and 82). Significantly, the commentary places this advice to the *therīs* in the mouth of the Buddha. There is, however, a crucial difference in the content of the advice. While the Buddha advises Vaṅgīsa, the *thera*, to see the 'constituent elements' (i.e., the body) as other, he advises Nandā, the *therī*, to see the unpleasant body as herself (83). Nowhere in the *Therīgāthā* are the *therīs* directly advised to abstract an unpleasant vision of the body away from themselves. Instead, they internalize it and encourage others to project disgust onto their own female bodies.

This feeling of disgust appears to be a necessary realization that impels the *therīs* and *theras* towards liberation. When everything is considered absolutely disgusting, they neither desire nor believe anything to have intrinsic beauty or value. In this way, they free themselves from the suffering that results from desiring something that is baseless and impermanent.

Looking at the Doctrine as a Mirror

Ideally, Buddhist practitioners should internalize this disgust for the body and recognize that all individuals are composite and impermanent, including themselves. This is the theory underlying the corpse meditation. Nothing could be as effective an illustration of transience and dissolution as witnessing the gradual decomposition of a human body. If all bodies are similarly constructed, then there really is nothing tangible one could regard as a self.

As we have seen, however, the *theras* do not internalize the view of the putrefying corpse nor do they treat the artificiality of their own physical beauty as an object of meditation, but they do tend to personalize the lesson of impermanence. Both the *therīs* and *theras* report the realization of the transient nature of their own bodies as the final step to attaining liberation.

The *Therīgāthā* contains five references to the *therīs* developing this notion of their own physical impermanence as the final realization leading to liberation. Dhammā describes herself weakly gathering alms then falling to the ground, 'having seen peril in the body', as her mind was completely released (17). Aḍḍhakāsī does not see peril in the body, but she describes her renunciation of prostitution as a result of her disgust and concomitant disinterest with her figure which led to her liberation (26). Abhayā Therī announces her decision to 'throw down this body' in response to a short warning: 'fragile is the body, to which ordinary individuals are attached' (35). The final example, Nanduttarā's poem, refers to her religious activities prior to her conversion to Buddhism as 'ministering to the body' (89). Her conversion and subsequent liberation is the result of her 'seeing the body as it really was' (90).

Again, though, Nandā's poem (see Rhys Davids' translation in the opening quote) provides us with the best example of a *therī* attaining liberation as a result of discovering the true nature of her own body. After Nandā is advised to view a decomposing body and consider its similarities with her own, she attains her goal:

> By (this same) me, vigilant, reflecting in a reasoned manner, this body was seen as it really was, inside and out.
>
> Then I became disgusted with the body, and I was disinterested internally. Vigilant, unfettered, I have become stilled, quenched. (*Therīgāthā* 85–86)

In the *Theragāthā*, there are seven references to *theras* contemplating their own bodies, none of which are as vivid as Nandā's. Two of the references are very abstract: both Sītavaniya and Soṇa Koḷivisa report the necessity of practicing 'mindfulness concerning the body' for one seeking the goal of liberation (6 and 636). Adhimutta's poem is somewhat less abstract, but still lacks a detailed explanation as to why he is discontented with his body:

> I am dissatisfied with the physical frame; I am not concerned with existence. This body will be broken, and there will not be another. (*Therīgāthā* 718)

Similarly, Tālapuṭa rhetorically questions when he will realize the utter impermanence of the body, and thereby attain his goal (1093).

The final three *theras* who contemplate their own bodies use stock references to 'looking at the doctrine as a mirror' and perceiving the emptiness of their own bodies (169–70, 171–72, and 395–96). Interestingly, the last of these examples, Kulla's poem, describes his contemplation as resulting from his meditation upon a female corpse in the cemetery. This is the only reference in the text in which a *thera* transfers the lesson of impermanence from the female body onto himself.

This is not, though, the only example of a *thera* attaining liberation as a result of viewing a female body. Four other *theras*, Nāgasamāla (267), Candana (299), Rājadatta (315), and Sundarasamudda (459), record their attainment of liberation as following immediately after their encounter with women. Significantly, they all report their response to the encounter as a realization of the peril of, and concomitant feeling of disgust with, the world. These *theras* attain liberation as a direct result of combatting their desire for the female body. They are tempted, but they recall the images of oozing putrefaction, and are repelled. Rājadatta's description of his desire for a female corpse is particularly revealing of this tendency:

> I, a *bhikkhu*, going to a burial ground, saw a woman cast away, thrown away in a cemetery, being eaten, full of worms.
>
> Seeing her, dead and evil, some men were disgusted. (But in my case) desire for sensual pleasures arose. Truly I was as though blind with regard to the flowing (body).
>
> Quicker than the cooking of rice I left that place. Possessed of mindfulness, attentive, I sat down on one side.
>
> Then reasoned thinking arose in me; the peril became clear; disgust with the world was established. (*Theragāthā* 315–318)

None of the *therīs* report their attainments as the result of seeing a man, alive or dead. Instead, their disgust with the world is the effect of viewing their own bodies. Again we see the essential difference between the texts' portrayals of the body: where the *therīs* personalize doctrinal conceptions of the body as impure and impermanent, the *theras* abstract these conceptions, projecting them onto others. When the *theras* do transfer their meditations onto their own bodies, their descriptions are less vivid and emotionally compelling and concentrate on their bodily emptiness rather than on the secretions and inner components of the body. These latter features of the body are reserved, on the whole, for women's bodies.

That is not to say, however, that the *theras* ignore their own aging processes. Here again, though, we find more detail and emotional resonance in the *therīs*' verses. The *Theragāthā* contains eleven references to bodily aging or illness.[21] Of those, seven are very abstract. The poems attributed to Uttiya (30), Kimbila (118), Kātiyāna (411), Sirimaṇḍa (447), Bhūta (518), and Tālapuṭa (1093) record abstract homilies on the pervasiveness of death, disease, and old age. Sirimaṇḍa's verse is a good example of this abstraction:

> Death, disease, old age, these three approach like huge fires. There is no strength to comfort them; there is no speed to run away.

> One should make one's day not unproductive, whether by a little or by much. Every (day and) night one passes, one's life is less by that much. (*Theragāthā* 450–451)

There are, however, four references that do provide us with some feeling for the authors. Dhammasava's father claims to have been one hundred twenty years old when he renounced (108); Jambuka describes his fifty-five years of extreme austerities prior to his conversion to Buddhism (283); Sappadāsa reports twenty-five years of renunciation that culminates in a suicide attempt (405); and Ānanda describes serving the Buddha with loving deeds, words and thoughts for the twenty-five years he was a learner (1039–1043).

The *Therīgāthā* contains ten poems in which the *therīs* refer to aging or illness.[22] Of these, only one attains the kind of abstraction typical of the *Theragāthā*. In Sumedhā's long speech to her parents on the evils of sensual pleasures, she refers to aging in abstract terms reminiscent of the *theras*' homilies: 'When old age and death are following closely one must strive for their destruction' (493). Towards the end of the poem, she states that all births are bound up with old age, death, and sickness (511).

The remaining nine references in the *Therīgāthā* convey some feeling for the ascribed authors. Cittā (27) and Mettikā (29) report being sick and weak as they climb a mountain and attain the goal. Another Sāmā (39) and A Certain Unknown *Bhikkhunī* (67) open their poems with the statement that they have been renunciants for twenty-five years before they obtained their liberation. Sumanā, Mittakālī, Soṇā, and Bhaddā the former Jain report being old and provide some detail about their experiences of aging: Sumanā's poem bids her to sleep happily, calling her 'old lady' (16); Mittakālī recognizes that her life is short and being destroyed by old age and sickness (95); Soṇā's age is highlighted by the ten sons she records having borne (102); and Bhaddā's age is expressed by the fifty-five years she reports having eaten almsfood (110).

Of the references to the aging process, the poem attributed to Ambapālī in the *Therīgāthā* is by far the most vivid in either text. Each of its nineteen verses is entirely devoted to a comparison of the features of her body when she was youthful and beautiful with those now that she is old and no longer beautiful. The poem begins with her hair and moves down her body through her face, arms, body, and feet, concluding with an overall assessment of her body. Each component is analyzed separately and in a detached fashion, alternating a description of youthful perfection with aged decay:

> My hair was black, like the colour of bees, with curly ends; because of old age it is like bark-fibres of hemp; not otherwise is the utterance of the speaker of truth. (*Therīgāthā* 252)

> Formerly my hands looked beautiful, possessing delicate signet rings, decorated with gold; because of old age they are like onions and radishes; not otherwise is the utterance of the speaker of truth. (*Therīgāthā* 264)

> Formerly both my feet looked beautiful, like (shoes) full of cotton-wool; because of old age they are cracked, and wrinkled; not otherwise is the utterance of the speaker of truth.
>
> Such was this body; (now) it is decrepit, the abode of many pains; an old house, with its plaster fallen off; not otherwise is the utterance of the speaker of truth. (*Therīgāthā* 269–270)

Siegfried Lienhard has shown that the first section of each verse, describing her youthful body, uses images from secular poetry contemporary, he argues, with the texts.[23] The Buddhist adaptation of this poetry, seen in the closing phrase of each description, involves juxtaposing a romantic (secular) vision of eternal beauty with a medical (Buddhist) vision of the body as it has aged.[24] This juxtaposition is clearly a meditation on impermanence using the body of a courtesan renowned in Buddhist literature for her beauty.[25] Although Ambapālī nowhere in the poem refers to her attainment of liberation, she has clearly looked at the doctrine as a mirror; she sees the truth of impermanence reflected in her own experience of aging.

Thus we find, yet again, that the *therīs* internalize the doctrine of aging. While the *theras* also internalize it, they do not do so as vividly or as personally. In their meditations of bodily impermanence, the *therīs* turn to their own experiences of aging and illness. In contrast, the *theras* show a marked preference for abstract homilies outlining the human condition as one of inevitable decay, but they refrain from examining their own physical processes of decay. Though, in this case, the *theras* do not project their perceptions of the body onto others, they also do not explore the implications of these perceptions in their own lives. The fact that the *Therīgāthā* devotes a whole poem of nineteen verses to Ambapālī's aging indicates the text's greater readiness to portray the *therīs*' identification of doctrine with their own bodies.

These differences indicate that the doctrinal emphasis on the necessity of overcoming attachment to the body is interpreted differently by the *therīs* and *theras*. The *therīs* view the problem of the body as an attachment to self that is to be overcome by examining their own life-histories and biological processes. The *theras* view the problem of attachment as desire for other which is to be overcome by projecting images of the true nature of the body as disgustingly impure onto others.

These differing interpretations explain, in part, why the *therīs* perceive liberation in terms of struggle. Overcoming the attachment to a false conception of the body is difficult for both *therīs* and *theras*. Regardless, the *therīs*' struggle against the false conception of self is much more immediate and personal than the *theras*' struggle against a false conception of other. Furthermore, the methods by which the authors conquer their delusions must be different. Since the object of the *therīs*' struggle is internal, it cannot be escaped, but must be faced; no matter what they do, the *therīs* remain embodied. In contrast, the object of the *theras*' struggle is external, it can be escaped. And, as we shall see in the next chapter, it is escape that is advocated by the *theras*.

CHAPTER IV

Looking Outward: Attitudes Towards The Physical Environment

> If there be none in front, nor none behind who can be found, alone and in the woods Exceedingly pleasant doth his life become. Come then! alone I'll get me hence and go To lead the forest-life the Buddha praised, And taste the welfare which the brother knows, Who dwells alone with concentrated mind. Yea, swiftly and alone, bound to my quest, I'll go to the jungle that I love, the haunt Of wanton elephants, the source and means of thrilling zest to each ascetic soul.
>
> Ekavihāriya, *Theragāthā*, 537–39[1]

There is a contention among some scholars that the earliest phase of Buddhism was one in which the Buddha and his disciples lived an eremitic lifestyle, wandering in the wilderness, coming into urban centers only to gather alms. They sometimes wandered alone, but, like other ascetic groups of the time, often gathered together for their forest-dwelling. These groups convened under a sheltered roof only for the annual monsoon when climatic conditions made outdoor living impossible. However, as Buddhism developed at least some of the Buddhist renunciants began to remain in these dwellings (*vihāras*) year round.[2]

This lifestyle of wilderness-dwelling is assumed in several the earliest collections of Buddhist *gāthā*. Many texts refer to *bhikkhus*' solitary meditations in the wilderness using beautiful and vivid images of the natural environment. For example, the *Khaggavisāṇasutta* in the *Suttanipāta* extols the virtue of one living alone and wandering in the forest, like the horn of a rhinoceros:[3]

> Like an unbound deer in the forest seeks a feeding-place when it will, wise, considering independence, one should live, alone, like the horn of a rhinoceros.

The concept of renunciation itself echoes this emphasis on living apart from civilization and the entanglements of social life. In 'going forth to the homeless life' (*pabbajiṃ anagāriyaṃ*), the Buddhist ascetic explicitly renounces home and family to embrace a lifestyle apart from the comforts of culture. Metaphorically, this leaving the home is equated with abandoning concepts of self; the house is frequently used as a symbol of a false sense of individuality. Leaving it is therefore freeing oneself of this false notion and realizing the composite nature of one's own self.[4]

The image of the Buddha's enlightenment also conveys a reverence for the natural environment. In the famous accounts of his biography,[5] he left his home to pursue a life of asceticism, which proved ultimately ineffective. He then sat down at the foot of a tree, vowing not to leave until he had attained liberation. As we shall see, the *Therīgāthā* and *Theragāthā* contain numerous instances of the *therīs* and *theras* following his example and attaining their own liberation as they meditate at the foot of a tree. Likewise, the two texts unanimously commend leaving the household for the homeless life, sometimes using this imagery to convey liberation itself. The texts differ, however, in the extent to which they revere the natural environment. Like many of the early *gāthā* collections, the *Theragāthā* frequently portrays the *theras* alone in wilderness settings, revelling in their solitude, but the *Therīgāthā* contains far less nature imagery. The *therīs* occasionally go to the forest to meditate, but the collection as a whole contains no explicit meditations on the beauty of the natural environment, nor do the *therīs* glorify solitude.

The reason for this difference may have been that by the time of the *Therīgāthā*'s composition, *bhikkhunīs* had been prohibited from living in the forest. I.B. Horner informs us that the ordination ceremony for women prescribed in the *Vinaya* includes only three of the four conditions of renunciation permitted for men: almsfood (*pindiyālopabhojana*), a robe made from rags taken from a garbage (*paṃsukūlacīvara*), and decomposing urine as medication (*pūtimuttabhesajja*). The condition omitted from the *bhikkhunīs*' list is permission for them to dwell at the foot of a tree (*rukkhamūlasenāsana*).[6]

Horner thinks that this omission relates to the rape of the *bhikkhunī* Uppalavaṇṇā while she was dwelling in the forest.[7] In order to protect *bhikkhunīs* from similar attacks, the Buddha instituted new rules restricting them to communal dwellings. As confirmation for this restriction, Horner cites the *Vinaya* account of the Buddha requesting King Pasenadi to build a *vihāra* for the *bhikkhunīs* within the city walls.[8]

These examples from the *Vinaya* indicate that the *bhikkhunīs* did dwell in the wilderness early in the history of the *sangha*, although none of the *therīs* report doing so. In fact, several of the *therīs* describe a long period of wandering that seems to end when they joined the *bhikkhunī-sangha* (e.g., Nanduttarā [87], Candā [122], and Vāsiṭṭhī [133]). Ironically, they all refer to their conversion as 'going forth to the homeless state' (*pabbajiṃ anagāriyaṃ*).

Scholars studying the texts have noted that the abundance of nature imagery in the *Theragāthā* and the relative paucity of nature imagery in the *Therīgāthā* is one of the most striking differences between the texts. These studies have resulted in various explanations of why this difference should exist. C.A.F. Rhys Davids hypothesizes that women's socialization in ancient India would discourage women from seeking solitude in the woods.[9] Similarly, Winternitz cites Oldenberg's contention that the *theras*' emphasis on forest-dwelling is naturally not emphasized by the *therīs*. Unfortunately, he does not inform us why this 'natural' difference should exist.[10]

Most ingenious, however, is I.B. Horner's apologetic explanation. Arguing that the paucity of nature imagery reflects the *therīs*' general lack of concern with sensations, she states that women were not immune to the beauty of natural phenomenon,

> But it was because in meditation they concentrated more intensely than men, and shut away all distracting sights and sounds by an effort of the will, determined to sunder the bonds that dragged them backward to the hither shore. In order to reach the goal these women managed to restrain the senses, and for this reason the moment of attainment and its expression (*aññā*) are free from all sensory images.[11]

In other words, Horner sees the *therīs* as somehow more concentrated and less easily distracted than the *theras*.

Whether we accept these scholarly explanations or not, the differences between the texts' presentations of images of the natural environment need to be explained. We really cannot know if the differences derive from the differing types of dwellings inhabited by the authors of the texts, though we can argue for the plausibility of such a contention. What we can establish, however, is that the differences reveal a differing perspective from which the authors viewed their surroundings. In this chapter, therefore, I am interested in comparing the texts' use of images from the *therīs*' and *theras*' surroundings.

The Environment as Setting and Symbol

Though the goals of this chapter are consistent with the goals of the preceding chapters, the method employed herein is slightly different. The volume and complexity of images of the authors' surroundings prohibit a detailed study of each type of image. Therefore, I have prepared detailed charts of the most common images used in both texts (see Appendix C), but will analyze in the next section only one set of imagery, that of trees, as representative of tendencies in usage in the texts.

In the course of my analysis, I make two kinds of distinctions between the images. First, I identify whether the image is used as a setting for the ascribed author or as a symbol representing something other than itself. In the setting category I include references to images of the surroundings as settings for the authors, their anecdotes, and their examples.[12] In the symbol category, I include images used as metaphors, similes, and analogies.

Secondly, I evaluate whether the particular image is used positively (+), negatively (-), or ambivalently (*). My main criteria for evaluation is an assessment of whether or not the image is conducive to, or expressive of, meditation or liberation (+), inconducive to meditation or liberation (-), or ambivalent with regards to liberation (*).

For example, the *Theragāthā* contains many verses describing the beauty of the wilderness and the desirability of dwelling there for a person in quest of liberation. These verses from Bhūta's poem are typical:

> When in the sky the thunder-cloud rumbles, full of torrents of rain all around on the path of birds, and the *bhikkhu* who has gone into the cave meditates, he does not find greater contentment than this.
>
> When seated on the bank of rivers covered with flowers, with garlands of variegated woodland plants, happy indeed he meditates, he does not find greater contentment than this.
>
> When at night in a lonely grove, while the sky (-deva) rains, the fanged animals roar, and the *bhikkhu* who has gone into the cave meditates, he does not find greater contentment than this.
>
> When having kept his own thoughts in check, inside a mountain, having taken refuge in a mountain cleft, rid of distress and rid of barrenness of mind he meditates, he does not find greater contentment than this. (*Theragāthā* 522–525)

Because these images describe the surroundings of a *bhikkhu* in meditation, I identify all these images as positive settings. Other settings, however, are clearly not so positive. For example,

Mahānāma's one-verse poem in the *Theragāthā* also contains a reference to a mountain scene, but it is negative rather than positive:

> You are found wanting by the mountain with its many shrubs and trees, the famous Mt. Nesādaka with its covering. (*Theragāthā* 115)

I also designate as negative those settings of unliberated individuals, particularly when their setting implies practices that, from a Buddhist perspective, impede one's progress towards liberation. For example, Nanduttarā's poem in the *Therīgāthā* describes her ascetic practices prior to joining the *sangha* as ministering to her body (89). As part of her condemnation, she describes a river setting:

> I used to revere fire, and the moon, and the sun, and *devatās*. Having gone to river-fording-places, I used to go down into the water. (*Therīgāthā* 87)

Here the context makes the setting of Nanduttarā's anecdote clearly inconducive to her liberation: the religious practices she performed by the river are futile, at least from her perspective upon joining the Buddhist *sangha*.

Nanduttarā's poem also provides an example of the distinction I make between images used as settings and as symbols. The images of fire, moon, and sun do not describe the setting in her poem. Like many other *therīs* and *theras*, Nanduttarā refers to them to imply something else. Because they are used this way, I designate the images as 'symbols'. Furthermore, because they, like the river, refer to non-productive religious practices, I categorize them as negative.

Fire, moon, and sun, however, are not always used negatively. For example, Nadīkassapa's poem in the *Theragāthā* is very similar to Nanduttarā's. Like her, he presents his previous religious affiliation as misguided. Unlike her, he makes a pun about the fire he used to revere:

> I have eliminated my wrong view; all existences have been torn asunder. I (now) sacrifice to the fire which really merits a gift; I revere the Tathāgata. (*Theragāthā* 343)

In this case, the fire is clearly a positive symbol; it represents the Buddha himself.

Other images are not clearly positive or negative. These I designate as ambivalent since they often have nothing to do with liberation. For example, the village or city is used in both texts as a locus of temptation (-) and of liberation (+). However, in Isidāsī's poem, the city of Ujjeni simply provides the setting for her first marriage (*Therīgāthā* 405). Since her marriage has little to do with her liberation, in this case, I have identified the image of city as ambivalent (*). Similarly, I categorize as ambivalent those images used as symbols to which the referents are obscure or confused. For example, in searching for an appropriate simile for the Buddha's *nibbāna*, Sāriputta confesses himself stumped:

> Even the great sea, the earth, a mountain, and the wind are not applicable in simile to the teacher's excellent release. (*Theragāthā* 1013)

I designate these images as ambivalent because they do not adequately convey the greatness of liberation, though clearly they represent Sāriputta's best effort.

Following these criteria, I have counted and categorized the most common images used in both texts as setting and symbol. My findings, documented in Appendix C, are condensed in Table 3. As the Table illustrates, these images are used frequently in each text, both as setting and as symbol. Differences between the texts are immediately apparent though. The *theras*' most frequent settings are in the wilderness: in the forest, on mountains, surrounded by wild animals and rain, dwelling in huts. The least common settings are those associated with culture: the *theras* never use tame animals to describe a setting, nor do they refer frequently to houses, cities, or even *vihāras*.

TABLE III

Images of the Surroundings

	Therīgāthā		Theragāthā	
Image	Setting	Symbol	Setting	Symbol
Forest or Trees	+6 −9 *1 — 16	+0 −4 *3 — 7	+63 −5 *1 — 69	+6 −10 *1 — 17
Mountain & Rocks	+6 −0 *0 — 6	+0 −4 *0 — 4	+33 −2 *0 — 35	+8 −3 *2 — 13
Wild Animals	+0 −4 *0 — 4	+2 −11 *2 — 15	+27 −2 *0 — 29	+16 −19 *0 — 35
Tame Animals	+0 −7 *0 — 7	+2 −1 *0 — 3	+0 −0 *0 — 0	+14 −5 *0 — 19
Elephants (Wild or Tame)	+2 −3 *0 — 5	+1 −4 *1 — 6	+5 −1 *1 — 7	+24 −8 *0 — 32

	Therīgāthā		Theragāthā	
Image	Setting	Symbol	Setting	Symbol
Rain or Rainy Season	+0 –0 *0 — 0	+1 –1 *0 — 2	+26 –0 *3 — 29	+3 –4 *2 — 9
Flowing Water	+3 –3 *0 — 6	+1 –4 *0 — 5	+13 –1 *1 — 15	+4 –9 *4 — 17
Flood or Bog	+0 –0 *0 — 0	+0 –2 *0 — 2	+0 –0 *0 — 0	+1 –18 *0 — 19
Darkness or Night	+8 –0 *0 — 8	+0 –14 *0 — 14	+6 –4 *1 — 11	+0 –10 *1 — 11
Day, Sun, Moon, or Fire	+1 –1 *0 — 2	+2 –10 *0 — 12	+1 –2 *0 — 3	+27 –6 *0 — 33
Hut	+0 –0 *0 — 0	+0 –0 *0 — 0	+16 –0 *1 — 17	+1 –6 *1 — 8

	Therīgāthā		Theragāthā	
Image	**Setting**	**Symbol**	**Setting**	**Symbol**
Vihāra or Cell	+4 –4 *0 — 8	+0 –0 *0 — 0	+9 –2 *0 — 11	+0 –0 *0 — 0
House or Palace	+6 –3 *5 — 14	+1 –2 *1 — 4	+4 –2 *0 — 6	+1 –11 *5 — 17
Village or City	+6 –4 *2 — 12	+0 –0 *0 — 0	+6 –4 *2 — 12	+2 –1 *0 — 3

In contrast, the *therīs* refer relatively frequently to settings we would associate with culture. Like the *theras*, the *therīs* also refer most frequently to the forest, but subsequent references differ dramatically. Houses, cities, and *vihāras* follow the forest as the most frequent settings, while the wilderness situations common in the *Theragāthā* are relatively sparse in the *Therīgāthā*. The settings least frequently used in the *Therīgāthā* include wild animals, elephants and mountains. Significantly, none of the *therīs* mention huts, nor are any of them rained upon.

This difference in setting tends to confirm I.B. Horner's hypothesis that the *bhikkhunī-sangha* was restricted to communal dwelling. If, in fact, the *therīs* lived communally in *vihāras* close to towns and cities, we would expect them to focus more on cultured environments rather than on the wilderness. Likewise, if the *theras* did, in fact, live in wilderness retreats for at least part of the year, their poems would reflect this.

Table 3 has also revealed other, more remarkable differences in the frequency of occurrence and characteristic usage of several of the images. Condensing the table even further, we arrive at a striking difference in the relative proportions of positive and negative uses of the images both as settings and as symbols:

IMAGE AS SETTING

	Therīgāthā	*Theragāthā*
+	42 = 49.4%	209 = 85.7%
–	33 = 38.9%	25 = 10.2%
*	10 = 11.8%	10 = 4.1%
	85 = 100%	244 = 100%

IMAGE AS SYMBOL

	Therīgāthā	*Theragāthā*
+	10 = 11.6%	107 = 45.9%
–	66 = 76.8%	110 = 47.2%
*	10 = 11.6%	16 = 6.9%
	86 = 100%	233 = 100%

The *Therīgāthā* is significantly more prone to use images of the surroundings negatively both as setting and as symbol. In part, this reflects the differing tendencies we have already discovered between the texts. Many of the negative settings occur in the *therīs*' discussions of their pre-renunciation lifestyles, which, as we have seen, are relatively more numerous in the *Therīgāthā* than in the *Theragāthā* (see Chapter II). Also, as we have discovered repeatedly, conflict, which provides the context of many other negative settings, is much more frequent in the *Therīgāthā*.

I do not think these types of situations adequately explain the dramatically greater proportion of *therīs* who use environmental images negatively. Over seventy-five percent of the images used as symbols in the *Therīgāthā* are negative. In contrast, the *theras* tend to emphasize the positive aspects of their environment. Over eighty-five percent of the settings they describe are conducive to liberation (85.7%), and positive and negative symbols are used with almost the same frequency. In the *Therīgāthā*, positive settings are only slightly more frequent than negative, and negative symbols are over six times more numerous than positive.

We will turn now to a more detailed study of tree or forest imagery to attempt to discern patterns of expression that can help us understand this dramatic difference in emphasis between the texts.

Tree Meditations

The imagery of trees or forests is the most frequent setting referred to by both the *therīs* and the *theras*. These settings are also the most frequently described locations for *arahants* (see Appendix D). Trees or forests are, therefore, the most favorable settings in the texts. The *therīs* and *theras* often describe themselves meditating at the foot of a tree, strolling through the woods, or meeting with the Buddha in groves of trees.

In the *Theragāthā* we find several prescriptive passages describing the optimal psychological state and setting for the attainment of liberation. For example, Gotama's poem is clearly a recipe for liberation. Significantly, this poem refers to only one appropriate setting:

> Forest lodgings, secluded, with little noise, fit for a sage to resort to; this is fitting for an ascetic. (*Theragāthā* 592)

In another example, Sāriputta distinguishes between the setting of ordinary people and that of *arahants*:

> Whether in the village or in the forest, on low ground or on high, wherever the *arahats* live, that is delightful country.
>
> Forests are delightful, where (ordinary) people find no delight. Those rid of desire will delight there; they are not seekers after sensual pleasures. (*Theragāthā* 991–991)

That many of the *theras* follow these prescriptions is shown by the numerous references to liberated *theras* dwelling in the forest, or meditating at the foot of a tree. In the *Theragāthā*, fifteen of the authors describing themselves as liberated are situated in the forest or near trees during or subsequent to their attainment.[13] A very clear example of this is Ekavihāriya's ten-verse contemplation of the forest as a delightful and effective locus of liberation (see Rhys Davids' translation at the beginning of this chapter):

> If no-one else is found in front or behind, it is very pleasant for one dwelling alone in the wood.
>
> Come then, I shall go alone to the forest praised by the Buddha, which is pleasant for a resolute *bhikkhu* dwelling alone.
>
> Alone, pursuing my aim, I shall quickly enter the grove, which gives joy to sages, is delightful, and is haunted by rutting elephants. (*Theragāthā* 537–39)

In the *Theragāthā*, the forest is an overwhelmingly positive setting for those who wish to attain the religious goal: sixty-three of the sixty-nine references to forests or trees as setting are positive.

In the *Therīgāthā*, the forest is also the most frequent setting for *therīs* who are described as liberated,[14] but only six of the sixteen references to forests or trees as setting are clearly positive. Also, the text contains none of the prescriptive passages analogous to those in the *Theragāthā*. The closest comparable passage is in Subhā Kammāradhītā's poem in which an unnamed narrator advises us to look upon her as exemplary:

> See Subhā, the smith's daughter, standing (firm) in the doctrine. Having entered the immovable (state) she meditates at the foot of a tree. (*Therīgāthā* 362)

Despite the paucity of prescriptive passages, we do find eight of the *therīs* who describe themselves as liberated portrayed in the forest or near trees during or subsequent to their attainment. Also, they use similar terminology to that of the *theras* to describe themselves. For example, after contrasting her former life as a courtesan, Vimalā says:

> Today (that same) I, having wandered for alms with shaven head, clad in the outer robe, am seated at the foot of a tree, having obtained (the stage of) non-reasoning.
>
> All ties, those which are divine and those which are human, have been cut out. Having annihilated all the *āsavas*, I have become cool, quenched. (*Therīgāthā* 75–76)

Similarly, we find the forest to be a desirable location for the experience itself. However, while the *theras* are referred to as dwelling in the forest, the *therīs* are depicted as going out to the forest. For example, in the *Theragāthā*, Sunīta's verse intimates that the Buddha himself had recommended the forest as a suitable dwelling place:

> Dwelling alone in the forest, not relaxing, I myself performed the teacher's bidding, just as the conqueror had exhorted me. (*Theragāthā* 626)

This reference to Sunīta 'dwelling alone' is repeated very frequently in the *Theragāthā*: thirteen of the *theras* describe themselves in settings that include a hut (*kuṭika*) in which they live.[15] Many of these employ beautiful images of rain, rivers, mountains, and wild animals, to describe the wilderness that surrounds them. The tone in these poems is one of solitude, contemplation, and established residence. The *theras* appear firmly established in their wilderness retreats. For example, Añjanāvaniya's verse stresses the permanence of his location:

> Making a small hut, plunging into the Añjana forest, I dwelt there. The three knowledges have been obtained, the Buddha's teaching has been done. (*Theragāthā* 55)

In contrast, the *Therīgāthā* never uses the term 'hut', never describes rain or the rainy season, and never presents the *therīs* as dwelling in the wilderness.

The *therīs* do occasionally enter the woods, sometimes the same woods identified by the *theras*. For example, Sujātā's liberation experience occurs in the Añjana forest. Sujātā describes herself as enjoying herself in her pleasure garden when she is attracted to a *vihāra*:

> Having delighted there, having played, coming (back) to my own house, I saw a *vihāra*. I entered the Añjana wood at Sāketa.
>
> Having seen the light of the world, having paid homage (to him), I sat down. In pity (that same) one with vision taught me the doctrine.
>
> And having heard the great seer, I completely pierced the truth. In that very place I attained the stainless doctrine, the state of the undying. (*Therīgāthā* 147–149)

While this forest is clearly a positive setting for the authors' attainment of liberation in both texts, the emphasis differs: Añjanāvaniya, the *thera*, is firmly located within the forest, having built a hut to live in; Sujātā, the *therī*, is firmly located in her house (146). Her sojourn with the forest is brief, but productive. Also, her initial attraction is to the *vihāra*, which is not mentioned in Añjanāvaniya's poem. Moreover, the compiler (or perhaps the author) chose to associate the name of the *thera*, 'Añjanāvaniya', very closely with the name of the forest, 'Añjana', while the *therī*'s name reflects no such association.

The *Therīgāthā* does, however, contain one instance of the association between a *therī*'s name with a forest. Like Añjanāvaniya, Subhā Jīvakambavanikā's name is identical with the forest in which her poem is set, but, unlike him, the forest for her is the locus of confrontation. While she is on her way to the forest to meditate, a rogue obstructs her path and attempts to seduce her:

> You are young and not ugly; what will going-forth do for you? Throw away your yellow robe. Come, let us delight in the flowery wood.
>
> The towering trees send forth a sweet smell in all directions with the pollen of flowers; the beginning of spring is a happy season; come, let us delight in the flowery wood.

> At the same time the trees with blossoming crests cry out, as it were, when shaken by the wind. What delight will there be for you if you plunge alone into the wood?
>
> You wish to go without companion to the lonely, frightening, great wood, frequented by herds of beasts of prey, disturbed by cow-elephants, who are excited by bull-elephants.
>
> You will go about like a doll made of gold, like an *accharā* in Cittaratha. O incomparable one, you will shine with beautiful garments of fine muslin, with excellent clothes.
>
> I should be under you command if we were to dwell inside the grove; for there is no creature dearer to me than you, o *kinnari* with pleasant eyes. (*Therīgāthā* 370–375)

We notice immediately the vividness of the temptation and the repeated allusions to the forest. The forest imagery itself is very sensual and is intimately entwined with the rogue's sexual innuendo: the smell of the trees' fertility pervades the setting; they cry out as the wind shakes their flowers; and the wood is frequented with cow-elephants who are excited by bull-elephants.

In particular, though, we should note the rogue's request that she 'dwell inside the grove' with him (375). This is the only reference in the *Therīgāthā*, positive or negative, to even the possibility of a *therī* dwelling in the woods; clearly, the suggestion is not conducive to, or expressive of, her liberated state.

Furthermore, as we noted above in our analysis of relationships in the *sangha* (see Chapter II), Subhā's rogue emphasizes her solitude. Uppalavaṇṇā's poem in the *Therīgāthā* also presents a confrontation between a 'rogue' and a *therī* who is alone in the woods. In this case, though, Uppalavaṇṇā recognizes her adversary as Māra:

> 'Going up to a tree with a well-flowered top, you stand there alone at the foot of the tree; you have not even any companion; o child, are you not afraid of rogues?'

> Even if 100,000 rogues like you were to come together, I should not move a hair's breadth, I should not even shake. What will you alone do to me Māra? (*Therīgāthā* 230–231)

In both poems, the forest is presented as a dangerous location for women alone. The suggestion in the introduction to this chapter that *bhikkhunīs* were prohibited from forest-dwelling because of the possibility of rape is supported by these poems. Though the *therīs* do not dwell in the forest, but have gone into the wood alone to meditate, they are, nonetheless, accosted by rogues whose advances can easily be interpreted as threatening.

When we look to the *Theragāthā* for comparable passages, we find a striking difference. There are three confrontations between the *theras* and adversaries that occur in the forest. The first two are practically identical (350–54 and 435–40). In both, an unnamed adversary questions the *thera*'s capacity to survive the harsh conditions of the forest:

> Brought low by colic, dwelling in the grove, in the wood, where there is a restricted food supply, where it is harsh, how will you fare, *bhikkhu*? (*Theragāthā* 350 and 435)

Each author responds that he will be able to withstand the harsh conditions by developing the 'constituents of enlightenment, the faculties, and the powers' (352 and 437). In other words, their progress along the path to liberation enables them to withstand hardship.

The type of difficulty encountered by the *therīs* and the *theras* differs dramatically. Uppalavaṇṇā's and Subhā's adversaries propose the dangers of human rogues to women alone in the flowering forest. In both cases the *therīs* are confronted with fear and potential violence. In contrast, the *theras*, Vakkali and Nhātakamuni, are confronted with the possibility of starvation–a non-human threat. Also, the threat is very abstract. Nowhere in the *Theragāthā* do we find the vivid imagery employed in Subhā's seduction scene.

The third forest encounter in the *Theragāthā* is also abstract and lacking in vivid detail. In this confrontation, Mahāmoggallāna directs an enigmatic tirade at an opponent identified as Māra in the last four verses. According to the commentary Māra has entered and then left the *thera*'s bowels.[16] After describing the adverse affects of assaulting a *bhikkhu*, Mahāmoggallāna rebukes Māra directly for assaulting the Buddha:

> Truly a fire does not think, 'I shall burn the fool', but the fool is burned having assailed that burning fire.
>
> Even so, Māra, having assailed the Tathagata you will burn yourself like a fool touching fire.
>
> Having assailed the Tathāgata Māra acquired demerit. Do you think, evil one, 'My evil is not maturing?'
>
> Evil is heaped up for you for a long time, as you do it, end-maker. Keep away from the Buddha, Māra; place no hope in *bhikkhus*.
>
> So the *bhikkhu* censured Māra in the Bhesakaḷa grove. Then that *yakkha*, dejected, vanished on the spot. (*Theragāthā* 1204–1208)

Māra does not directly propose a threat to Mahāmoggallāna. Instead, Mahāmoggallāna appears to pose a threat to Māra. Also, this account is much more abstract: there is no reference to Māra's attempted seduction or temptation of the *thera*. If we can accept the commentary, we should also note the repeated allusions to the *theras*' stomachs in these encounters. The *theras* Vakkali and Nhātakamuni are confronted with starvation, Mahāmoggallāna with indigestion. In contrast, the *therīs* Uppalavaṇṇā and Subhā are confronted with seduction, perhaps rape.

This contrast between the texts' relative degree of abstraction further highlights the *Therīgāthā*'s emphasis on the negative or undesirable consequences of their renunciation. Though both texts portray the forest as a desirable location for meditation and liberation, the *Therīgāthā* emphasizes the adverse conditions that are also present in the forest. In the *Therīgāthā*, nine of the sixteen references to forest settings are negative; in the

Theragāthā, only five of sixty-nine are negative. The *Therīgāthā* is clearly more prone to emphasize the unpleasant aspects of the lifestyle of renunciation and the quest for liberation.

We see this when we compare two almost identical poems from each text. Both texts contain an account of an ascribed author attempting suicide after several years of fruitless effort. In the *Therīgāthā*, Sīhā describes herself as desperately unhappy as she enters the forest to hang herself:

> Thin, pale, and wan, I wandered for seven years; (being) very pained, I did not find happiness by day or night.
>
> Then taking a rope, I went inside a wood, (thinking) 'Hanging here is better for me than that I should lead a low life again.'
>
> Having made a strong noose, having tied it to the branch of a tree, I cast the noose around my neck. Then my mind was completely released. (*Therīgāthā* 77–81)

Similarly, Sappadāsa's poem in the *Theragāthā* describes him as desperately attempting suicide (405–410). The structure of his poem is also remarkably similar to that of Sīhā: he is desperate after twenty-five years of renunciation, still afflicted with sensual pleasures, leaving his cell to sit on a couch with a knife. As he was about to cut his wrist, he attains the 'release of his mind'.

The difference in setting in these remarkably similar poems is very significant. While both poems stress the location of the authors' thoughts and suicide attempts (each poem mentions the location twice), the location differs: Sīhā, the *therī*, goes to a forest while contemplating her unhappiness, Sappadāsa, the *thera*, goes outside a cell; Sīhā ties her rope to a tree, Sappadāsa clutches his knife on a couch. The forest setting of Sīhā's desperation reveals the greater readiness of the *Therīgāthā* to describe the negative features of the authors' experiences. Although the forest is the preferred setting for meditation or liberation in both texts, the *Therīgāthā* is more willing to situate the most graphic example of desperation and struggle in the quest for liberation in the forest. In contrast, the *Theragāthā* never situates the *theras*' desperation or struggle in such a positive setting.

Envisioning the Environment

These examples confirm the general pattern in the texts' relative emphasis on negative usages of environmental imagery. The *Therīgāthā* is far more prone to present the *therīs*' difficulties, even in positive settings. Yet the *Therīgāthā* is also more likely to provide a setting for its liberated authors than is the *Theragāthā*. Of the fifty-six *therīs* who are described as liberated, twenty-four (42.9 percent) are situated in one or more of the settings I have analyzed. Only thirty-two of the ninety-seven liberated *theras* (33 percent) are described in one or more of these settings (see Appendix D). Thus, while the *Therīgāthā* has a greater proportion of its settings coinciding with liberated *therīs* it nonetheless favors negative usages of environmental imagery. The *Theragāthā* presents a lower proportion of its liberated authors in tangible settings, but tends to present settings positively.

This dramatic difference clearly relates to the differing emphasis on conflict we have already discovered in the texts. Those settings in which the *theras* or *therīs* encounter adversaries trying to tempt, frighten, or coerce them into activities or attitudes inconducive to liberation are, by definition, negative. Because the *Therīgāthā* contains such a greater proportion of confrontations, we should expect a greater proportion of negative settings.

The context of conflict, however, plays no role in the category of symbol. In distinguishing between positive and negative uses of environmental imagery as symbols, I have analyzed only the referents of the images. If a particular image refers to aspects of liberation, liberated individuals, or the ascribed author's realization of liberation, I categorize it as a positive symbol. If an image refers to impediments to liberation, unliberated individuals, or samsaric existence, I categorize it as a negative symbol. The particular context of the *therī* or *thera* who uses imagery in this way is completely irrelevant.

For example, frequently in both texts, fire symbolizes the cycle of *saṃsāra*, or aspects therein.[17] In the *Therīgāthā*, Nanduttarā (87), Paṭācārā (116), Sīsūpacālā (200), Subhā Jīvakambavanikā (387 and 398), and Sumedhā (488, 493, 504, and 507) use fire this way. Sīsūpacālā's verse is perhaps the most vivid expression of this:

> The whole world is ablaze, the whole world has flared up, the whole world is blazing, the whole world is shaken. (*Therīgāthā* 200)

Similarly, the *Theragāthā* contains many references to the 'fires' of *saṃsāra*. Kātiyāna (415 and 416), Udāyīn (720), Anuruddha (906), and Tālapuṭa (1099) use this symbolism in much the same way as the *therīs*. In particular, Tālapuṭa's verse is very close to Sīsūpacālā's as he rhetorically questions when he will attain a liberated perspective:

> When shall I, possessed of calmness, by wisdom see innumerable sights, and sounds, smells, tastes, things to touch, and mental phenomena as a blazing mass? When will this thought of mine be? (*Theragāthā* 1099)

The context of these verses is completely irrelevant to my identification of these images of fire as negative. Furthermore, as these examples indicate, the referents for many of the images used as symbols in the texts are very similar, but the *Therīgāthā* still contains a much higher proportion of negative images than the *Theragāthā*. In the *Therīgāthā*, 76.8 percent of all images used as symbols are negative. In the *Theragāthā*, only 47.2 percent of the images used as symbols are negative. If context is irrelevant, how, then are we to understand this difference?

In part, I think, the greater emphasis on positive symbolism in the *Theragāthā* can be attributed to the presence of usages foreign to the *Therīgāthā*. Looking again at images of fire used symbolically, we discover that the *Theragāthā* frequently compares the light of the fire with the brightness of liberating wisdom. Kaṅkhārevata (3), Nadīkassapa (343), Jenta Purohitaputta (426), Sāriputta (1014), and Mahāmoggallāna (1156, 1204, 1205) use fire imagery to illustrate the illuminating aspects of liberation. Kaṅkhārevata's one-verse poem is a clear example:

> See this wisdom of the Tathāgatas, who, giving light and vision like a fire blazing in the night, dispel the doubt of those who come. (*Theragāthā* 3)

The *Therīgāthā* never uses fire imagery in this way.

Thus, while both texts use this particular imagery in a similar fashion to exemplify the true nature of *saṃsāra*, the *Theragāthā* employs the same imagery to illustrate aspects of liberation. The *Theragāthā* transforms a negative image into positive usages. This confirms the *Theragāthā*'s generally positive worldview. In contrast, the *Therīgāthā*'s more negative worldview is unmitigated by such positive usages of symbols of the environment. I think we can interpret this tendency towards a positive or negative worldview as a consistent feature of the *Theragāthā* and *Therīgāthā*, respectively. As we have already seen in previous chapters, the *Therīgāthā* exhibits a greater concern with samsaric existence; with the suffering, passion, and disillusionment that characterize the existential condition of ordinary individuals. The *Theragāthā* is relatively unconcerned with the realm of *saṃsāra*: the *theras* do not discuss their prerenunciation experiences as frequently as the *therīs*; they condemn the foolishness of ordinary individuals rather than attempt to convert that foolishness into wisdom; and, they view the transience of all things as somehow 'other' than themselves – unlike the *therīs*, they do not meditate on their own bodies as insubstantial and impermanent. The *theras* thus tend to abstract the negative aspects of their quest for liberation away from themselves.

The settings most frequently described in the texts add additional confirmation to this tendency. The *theras*' wilderness locations provide them the opportunity to escape the manifestations of *saṃsāra* that could encourage attitudes and behaviors inconducive to their quest for liberation. They live in solitude, so they do not have to worry about impassioned social interactions; they see women only when they go for alms, so the external source of their desire is alleviated; they are distracted only by nature itself, which, although it might inspire feelings of awe and wonder, will not likely induce desire, hate, and envy. In contrast, the *therīs* are presented as living communally in *vihāras*. They must contend with potentially disruptive relationships, with their tendency to entangle themselves with other individuals. Though the *therīs*, like the *theras*, seek out forest locals to meditate, they may encounter threatening rogues there who interpret their solitude as sexual availability. The *therīs*, therefore, cannot escape the obstacles to liberation, but must confront them. The *theras* can, and apparently did, avoid such obstacles.

This, I think, can help us understand the difference in the texts' usage of environmental imagery as symbols. If we can accept the settings and situations described in the texts as relating to the actual experiences of the authors or compilers of the texts, we can interpret the tendencies towards a generally negative or positive worldview as a logical outcome. If the women who composed and preserved the *Therīgāthā* did, in fact, experience the kinds of difficulties to which the text alludes, we can expect them to project those difficulties into the realm of symbols.

CHAPTER V

Struggle for Liberation in the *Therīgāthā*

> How should the woman's nature hinder us? Whose hearts are firmly set, who ever move With growing knowledge onward in the Path? What can that signify to one in whom Insight doth truly comprehend the Norm? On every hand the love of pleasure yields, And the thick gloom of ignorance is rent In twain. Know this, O Evil One, avaunt! Here, O Destroyer! shalt thou not prevail.
>
> Somā, *Therīgāthā*, 61–62[1]

If, as I have argued, the *Therīgāthā* and *Theragāthā* were indeed designed as 'liberation manuals', as didactic models for the successful quest for liberation, we can conclude that the audience towards which they were directed was very diverse. The texts present us with a variety of methods for attaining liberation. Their diversity implies that anyone can attain liberation. The particular aspects of self that require transformation will be specific to our experiences, dispositions, and habitual tendencies. If we are afflicted with desire for sensual pleasures, the texts demonstrate with vivid images the true nature of the body. If we are overcome with grief, the texts illustrate the absolute transience of all things, and explain how we have grieved for thousands of lifetimes. If our determination and vigilance wanes after prolonged effort to attain liberation, the texts provide us with inspirational examples of others whose achievement follows a period of despair and frustration.

In short, the texts are directed to meet a great variety of needs. Clearly, the texts are designed to illustrate the various ways in which people have attained liberation, regardless of their initial state of mind, but, as we have seen, the terms, images, and situations they employ to create these models differ quite significantly between the texts. It is now time to compile and consolidate the differences we have discovered through our analysis of the texts.

Models of Liberation

Throughout this study, we have arrayed a variety of numerical differences in the use of terms, situations, and contexts between the texts. Most striking are differences in the percentage of ascribed authors referring to their own attainment of liberation (*Therīgāthā*, fifty-six of seventy-three or 76.7 percent; *Theragāthā*, ninety-seven of two hundred sixty-four or 36.7 percent); the number of verses devoted to overt conflict (*Therīgāthā*, one hundred eighty-four of five hundred twenty-two, or 35.2 percent; *Theragāthā*, seven of one thousand two hundred seventy-nine, or 0.5 percent); the number of ascribed authors describing previous lifestyles (*Therīgāthā*, twenty-five of seventy-three, or 34.2 percent; *Theragāthā*, twenty-five of two hundred sixty-four, or 9.5 percent) and referring to conversion (*Therīgāthā*, 23.3 percent; *Theragāthā*, 4.9 percent); the percentage of images of the surroundings used negatively as settings (*Therīgāthā*, 38.8 percent; *Theragāthā*, 10.2 percent) and as symbols (*Therīgāthā*, 76.8 percent; *Theragāthā*, 47.2 percent).

These numerical differences reflect and reinforce differences in thematic emphasis throughout the texts. In the analyses of renunciation, the body, and imagery of the surroundings above, we have attempted to uncover differences in the attitudes and assumptions of the authors of the two texts. The unifying theme running through these studies has been the *therīs*' emphasis on struggle and the *theras*' emphasis on escape in their quest for liberation. These differing emphases can now be compiled into three categories: the authors' attitudes towards relationships; the degree of personalization or abstraction they display; and their experiences of, and responses to, conflict.

Relationships have a prominent role in the *Therīgāthā*. In the chapter on renunciation, we discovered that the *therīs* tend to focus on relationships of all kinds: from their parenthood and the pain caused by the deaths of their children, to adversarial confrontations with others, to friendships in the *sangha* among the *bhikkhunīs*. In the chapter on the body, we found that many of the references to the ascribed author's own bodily processes were used to instruct adversaries on the futility of maintaining a romantic delusion of beauty. And, in the chapter on physical surroundings, we found that the *therīs* dwell communally in *vihāras*.

In contrast, the *theras* do not discuss their relationships with others as often or as vividly as the *therīs*. They never refer to grieving over the deaths of family members, nor do they acknowledge their renounced parenthood as openly or as frequently as the *therīs*. They refer to friendship only in abstract terms, and show a pronounced preference for dwelling in isolation. When they meet with the possibility of sexual encounters with women, they do not attempt to instruct the women on the error of their ways, but rather, hurl verbal abuses at them, condemning the desire they have induced as indicative of their unenlightened state.

These differing attitudes towards relationships indicate a differing understanding of the kind of detachment that characterizes a liberated individual. The *therīs* see themselves as continuing to interact positively with others, and interpret the unenlightened state as one in which relationships are fraught with deception, hatred, and contempt. For the *therīs*, detachment means a transformation of their emotional response to others. The *theras* also describe the liberated person as one who is imbued with compassion, but their recorded social interactions display little emotion. Instead of detachment from negative emotional states, the *theras*' social discourse reveals their psychological detachment from all emotional bonds with others in what amounts to a complete severing of relationships.

Repeatedly throughout our study we have noted the difference in levels of personalization and abstraction. In our analysis of technical terms, we discovered that a very high proportion of the *therīs* report their own liberation. Those *therīs* who discuss the liberation of others provide them with tangible personalities. In our study of renunciation, we found that the *therīs* describe their previous lifestyles in much more detail and with much more emotional resonance than the *theras*. In the study of the body, we found that the *therīs* appropriate the doctrine of the impurity, deception, and impermanence of the body by reflecting on their own physical experiences. And, throughout, we have seen the *therīs* detailing confrontations with adversaries who pose a clear and personal threat.

In contrast, the *theras* prefer abstract, non-personalized descriptions. They use the language of liberation to refer to others more frequently than to themselves, and those others are often idealized, hypothetical figures. They do not provide details of their previous lifestyles, nor do they describe their relationships in emotionally compelling detail. They do not reflect frequently or graphically upon the relevance of doctrine to their own physical experiences, and they project impure and deceptive features of the body onto others. Finally, their descriptions of overt conflict do not contain the personal threat contained in the *therīs*' descriptions, but rather represent impersonal forces that may be dangerous to their health.

The personalization of the *Therīgāthā* and the abstraction of the *Theragāthā* indicate that the authors understand central features of Buddhist doctrine differently. The *therīs* contemplate the doctrine of impermanence by reflecting upon their own life histories, their own experiences of relationships transforming, and their own bodies aging. They see the delusory perception of permanence and stability as it has been experienced in their own lives. They overcome the delusion by reflecting on their own experiences. The *theras* also know the delusion of permanence to be the main obstacle to their quest for liberation, but they contemplate the impermanence of others. They do not reflect on their own experience, but rather concentrate on the environment around them, abstracting impermanence away from themselves.

Thus we see that although both must overcome a false perception, their methods of doing so differ. The *therīs* internalize the obstacles and must combat them in their own psyches. The *theras* externalize the obstacles and conquer them by isolating themselves away from them.

The presence of overt conflict in the *Therīgāthā* is one of the most prominent features of the text. As we noted above, the text devotes a large percentage of its verses to descriptions of *therīs*' conflict with adversaries. In the study of renunciation, we discovered some evidence of conflict with family over the *therīs*' decision to renounce. Once renounced, they continue to encounter adversaries who attempt to frighten, seduce, or coerce them to give up their religious commitments. In the chapter on the body, we found that the *therīs*' internalization of doctrinal notions of feminine physicality makes their struggle to overcome an attachment to the false perception of self personal and immediate. Finally, we found that the *therīs*' living situation poses continual conflict for them. As they are already socialized to form deep attachments with others, the communal living could only serve to make the required transformation of emotional attachments a constant source of struggle. Furthermore, the forest, though a desirable setting for the attainment of liberation, poses the danger of disrespectful libertines threatening seduction or perhaps even rape.

The *theras* do not concentrate on conflict nearly as much as the *therīs*. The major source of their conflict, their sexual desires for women, is combatted by minimizing contact. They do not concentrate on their memories of the enjoyments or suffering they have experienced prior to renunciation, but instead, concentrate more on the joys of solitude. Their wilderness dwelling thus provides them with the opportunity to escape from the object of their desires. Indeed, the *theras* are often advised against approaching women at all. When they do encounter women on their daily begging for alms, they project images of post-mortem decay and oozing putrefaction upon the bodies of the women they desire.

Thus, we see that the texts' presentations of the experiences of renunciants differ significantly. The *Therīgāthā* is far more prone to discuss the negative repercussions of renunciation for the *therīs*: from their struggle to obtain permission to renounce, to their internal conflict with a false conception of self, to their conflicts with various adversaries presenting obstacles to their quest for liberation. Significantly, the *Therīgāthā* is also willing to devote a whole poem twenty verses long to a woman's attempted seduction of her renounced husband (291–311). The *Theragāthā*, in contrast, presents very few instances of overt conflict, though this example from the *Therīgāthā* indicates that the *theras* may have experienced more conflict than they tend to portray.

This remarkable difference implies a differing attitude towards liberation. While the *Therīgāthā* presents the quest of liberation as fraught with difficulties that must be faced, the *Theragāthā* underplays the difficulties and advocates escape rather than confrontation. These tendencies are also apparent in the texts' use of symbolism. The technical terms for liberation reflect each text's characteristic emphasis or de-emphasis on conflict and symbols of the environment are used negatively with much greater frequency in the *Therīgāthā* than the *Theragāthā*.

The models of liberation the texts present are thus very different. The model portrayed in the *Therīgāthā* is one of hardship and struggle; in the *Theragāthā*, it is one of peacefulness and quietude.

Striking though these differences are, however, they must be understood as very subtle. An initial reading of the texts gives one the impression of similarity rather than of difference between them. Both use identical terms and phrases to describe the goal of liberation, the liberation experience, and the attributes of those who have attained it. The most common structure of the poems is also identical. Both texts frequently employ the literary device of contrast to enhance the religious component of the poems: poetic descriptions of scenery, situation, and sentiment are frequently juxtaposed with religious expressions of realization, bliss, and joyful conquest over desire.[2]

The Question of Female Authorship

These similarities provide the basis of an argument for the common authorship of the texts. If we are to test the feasibility of this argument, I think we can discount the possibility of a woman, or group of women, as the author common to both texts. Given the generally denigrating portrayal of women's intellectual capacities throughout the Pali Canon, it is inconceivable that the tradition would accept women's accounts of male religiosity as authoritative. Yet, as Winternitz maintains, it is also highly unlikely that men would bother composing the verses of the *Therīgāthā* and attributing them to women:

> First of all, the monks never had so much sympathy with the female members of the community, as to warrant our crediting them with having composed these songs sung from the very hearts of women.... For the same reason it would never have occurred to the monks to ascribe songs to the women, if an incontestible tradition had not pointed at this direction.[3]

If we are to seriously doubt the female authorship of the *Therīgāthā*, we must assume male authorship. To be considered valid, this assumption would have to explain the subtlety and consistency of the differences we have discovered between the texts. By speculating on what a male author might have perceived as female concerns, we can attempt to determine if this possibility is at all feasible. The question then becomes one of determining the differences that could conceivably derive from the male impersonation of the *therīs*.

Of the differences outlined above, we could explain the *therīs*' emphasis on relationships as a male interpretation of typical female preoccupations with others. As we have seen in the chapter on renunciation, many of the relationships described in the *Therīgāthā* are stereotypically feminine: the *therīs* describe themselves as loyal wives, loving mothers, and grieving widows. The stereotypical nature of these depictions could easily derive from a general perception of female nature.

Likewise, the texts' portrayals of the female body's impurity and deceptiveness are remarkably similar. Ambapālī's poem emphasizing the decline in beauty of a beautiful courtesan could be part of a male meditation on the bodily decline of one of their sources of desire. Thus, the portrayals of the body in the *Therīgāthā* could reflect a male perspective.

Differences in setting could also be part of a male conception of female religious experiences. If, as the texts indicate, women were prohibited from dwelling in the wilderness, it would be natural for a male author to present the *therīs* in cultural settings.

Nevertheless, these possibilities are very superficial. They fail to account for the consistent and subtle differences we have discovered in our close reading of the *Therīgāthā*: the *therīs*' choice of technical terms for liberation to refer to themselves; their characterization of other liberated individuals and their concrete usage of the abstract concept 'fool'; their references to *bhikkhus*' parenthood and men's grieving; the presentation of friendships in the *bhikkhunī-sangha*; the *therīs*' greater emphasis on conversion; the *therīs*' failure to predict the deaths of those attracted to their bodies; their neglect of snake imagery, and their use of body imagery to instruct adversaries; the proportion of images of the surroundings used negatively as both setting and symbol; and, finally, the *therīs*' dramatic portrayal of conflict, both for themselves and for *bhikkhus*.

Thus we see that while a superficial reading of the texts could support the notion of a common (male) author, a deeper reading makes such a conclusion highly unlikely. I find it exceedingly difficult to believe that anyone could consistently maintain the subtlety of the differing perceptions we have discovered in the texts. Though the fact of difference alone does not necessarily prove the female authorship of the *Therīgāthā*, it does lend credibility to the traditional assumption that the text did, in fact, originate in the *bhikkhunī-sangha*.

Scholarship on gender differences in story-telling tends to confirm this. Kristin Wardetzky's thorough study of fairy tales composed by contemporary German children illustrates how gender differences pervade the kinds of stories girls and boys tell and the personality traits they attribute to male and female characters. For example, though both girls and boys present victims unanimously as female, girls never portray female characters as sword-wielding heroines.[4] Boys do present female protaganists engaging in war-like behavior, but in so doing, follow male models from well-known fairy tales. In Wardetzky's analysis, the boys' female protagonists are 'male heroes wearing a female mask.'[5] Whenever the female protagonists in the girls' stories use a sword, they do not use it violently to destroy an adversary, but to transform him or her into a 'good' character.[6] Finally, Wardetzky discovered a pervasive thematic difference in the stories she analyzed. While girls' stories most frequently involve a loving, or erotic relationship between the characters, the boys describe battle scenes with three times the frequency of girls' tales.[7]

Clearly, the gender differences experienced by girls and boys in Germany during the 1980's have influenced the way they tell stories. This is not unique to Germany in the modern age. In a detailed study of differences in the presentation of female and male religious experiences in medieval Europe, Caroline Walker Bynum has discovered dramatic differences in the narrative descriptions of women's religiosity written by women and by men.

In her comparison of biographies of the female saints, Bynum found that male biographers tend to project their expectations onto women's biographies. When women write their own biographies, a major theme is continuity with their own social, biological, and psychological experiences as women. When men write women's stories (even in situations where autobiographies are extant), the themes are crises and their resolution, liminality, and dramatic symbolic gender reversals.[8] Likewise, male biographers describe women as weak more than women do, and assume that women's religious experiences require verification by their adoption of masculine qualities – an assumption not found in biographies written by women.[9] In other words, the men of medieval Europe assumed that women's religious experiences and modes of religious expression would be symmetrical with those of men. Bynum's analysis of women's own writings, however, proves that this assumption is false.

In a study closer geographically and thematically to our own, John Stratton Hawley also illustrates the difficulty men have presenting women's religiosity. Studying the sixteenth century devotional poetry attributed to Mira Bai, a woman, and Sur Das, a man, Hawley has uncovered significant gender differences in their adoption of the perspective of the *gopīs* (the female cowherding consorts of Krishna).[10] Though Mira Bai and Sur Das are close chronologically and geographically, writing in the same genre of poetry, using the same vocabulary and imagery, their poems display consistent differences.

According to Hawley, Sur Das' poetry exhibits signs of strain in his impersonation of the female *gopīs*' perspective. Most significant for our purposes are Hawley's discoveries that while Mira refers frequently to tensions among female family members, Sur focusses on jealousies among the *gopīs* for Krishna's attention, a focus Hawley claims to be based on the real life family tensions discussed by Mira.[11] Furthermore, Mira's poetry contains many comparisons of the *gopīs* to women, mythological, or otherwise. In contrast, Sur more frequently compares the spirituality of the *gopīs* to masculine than to feminine models.[12]

And finally, in a comparison that is strongly reminiscent of our own findings, Hawley contends that Mira's poetry represents a union between the secular and the sacred while Sur's poetry keeps the boundary between them clear.[13]

Both Bynum's and Hawley's studies reveal that men are unable to present the subtleties of women's religious experiences even when their intention is to present women's biographies. When their intention is to actually impersonate women, they fare no better. For our purposes, these studies highlight the improbability of male impersonation of the *therīs*. We can conclude, therefore, that, in all likelihood, the *Therīgāthā* was composed by women, does represent a female perspective on the life of renunciation, and was probably designed as a model of liberation specifically for women.

Women's Struggle for Liberation

We can now attempt to explain the dramatic differences in perspective we have discovered throughout this study of the texts. As we have seen repeatedly in every category of analysis we employed, struggle pervades the experiences of the *therīs*. They must struggle to gain permission to renounce, to maintain their vows of celibacy, and to transform their emotional attachments to others. They must also struggle against a perception of self that is much more personal and immediate than the *theras*' struggle against the false perception of other. Finally, we found that they must struggle to locate themselves in settings conducive to meditation and experiences of liberation.

In confirmation of this theme of struggle, we also found the *Therīgāthā* presenting more of the negative features of renunciation for both women and men. The *therīs* portray much more conflict, refer much more frequently to the difficulties they encounter, and project a negative worldview onto their use of symbols of the environment. Clearly, the perspective of the *therīs* is oriented towards difficulty more than that of the *theras*.

I think the reason for this difference in perspective is the *Therīgāthā*'s female authorship. Those women in ancient India who chose to become *bhikkhunīs* faced difficulties unknown to their male counterparts. Their decision to lead a life of celibacy and contemplation completely inverted the gender-stereotypes of their cultural milieu. Instead of being content with the life of a married woman, brightened by the births of sons and overshadowed by the possibility of childless widowhood, these women chose to follow the path of religious renunciation. Instead of centering their lives on the needs of others, they concentrated on their own self-fulfillment, though they continued to help each other in the *sangha*.

Consequently, it is not surprising that the society at large should fail to respect the *bhikkhunīs*. They had renounced all the roles available to women that make them valuable in society. The *bhikkhus* had also renounced their socially valuable roles, but the established tradition of male asceticism gave their vocation more credibility.

Also, we must consider the possibility that the Buddha himself contributed to the difficulty faced by the *bhikkhunīs*. His hesitancy in opening the *sangha* up to women, the subservience he required as a condition for women's ordination, and his stipulation that women dwell communally because of the problem of rape contributed to the obstacles women faced. Furthermore, he does not figure as prominently in the *Therīgāthā* as in the *Theragāthā*. Perhaps he shared his culture's devaluation of women, even though he was willing to acknowledge their capacity to attain the highest goal.

The combined effect of social disrespect, enforced subordination and neglect by the Buddha is reflected in the *therīs*' conception of liberation as struggle. Yet they successfully overcame these obstacles. In their verses, we not only detect evidence of their difficulties, but also of their triumph. The *therīs* do not reflect an attitude of resentment and bitterness towards the social and religious establishment that discriminated against them, but a compassionate hope that the individuals caught in worldly life will eventually attain a more liberated perspective.

As a text that illustrates such an optimistic hope for the liberation of all of us, the *Therīgāthā* has a powerful message for today. The very existence of a text that makes no apologies for its focus on women's religious experience shows us that women's struggle for 'liberation' has been going on for a long time. And one group of women, at least, succeeded.

APPENDIX A

Technical Terms for Liberation

The following table contains the references and frequency of occurrence of the fifteen most common terms and phrases used in both the *Therīgāthā* and the *Theragāthā* as synonyms for liberation, in the order of their frequency of occurrence in the *Therīgāthā*. The references are cited according to verse number. My findings are summarized in Table 1, '15 Most Common Goal Referents.'

I have categorized the terms and phrases according to whether they refer to the religious attainments of 'authors' or 'others'. In distinguishing between these categories, I pay close attention to the person to whom attainment is attributed and to the verb-tense and verb-referent of the term or phrase. The terms or phrases I identify as referring to authors include statements by or about ascribed authors that utilize verbs in the past or present tense and their accompanying gerunds, relative clauses, and adjectival compounds. Those I define as referring to others are statements about persons other than the ascribed authors, or statements by or about ascribed authors that incorporate imperatives or future tenses. This distinction between author and other is summarized in Table 2, 'The Author-Other Distinction', and is discussed at length in Chapter I.

	Therīgāthā		Theragāthā	
Technical Term	Author	Other	Author	Other
Desire Gone	1, 15, 16, 18, 24, 34, 36, 38, 41, 53, 56, 90 91, 99, 105, 132, 140, 156, 158, 207, 208, 334, 341, 369, 385	14, 165, 167, 168, 204, 205, 275, 337, 458	20, 56, 79, 158, 161, 180, 191, 192, 298, 327, 338, 344, 378, 416, 466, 517, 843, 844, 845, 846, 847, 848, 849, 850, 851, 852, 853, 854, 855, 856, 857, 858, 859, 860, 861, 890, 1059, 1060, 1061, 1125	10, 18, 39, 40, 56, 74, 154, 282, 306, 313, 338, 401, 402, 418, 491, 519, 526, 596, 600, 641, 665, 673, 699, 704, 707, 711, 806, 808, 810, 812, 814, 816, 840, 923, 972, 992, 1008, 1012, 1092, 1094, 1105, 1162, 1163, 1214, 1216, 1224, 1275
TOTAL:	24	9	40	47

Appendix A: Technical Terms for Liberation

	Therīgāthā		Theragāthā	
Technical Term	Author	Other	Author	Other
Rebirth Ended	11, 22, 47, 56, 65, 91, 106, 149, 158, 160, 221, 334, 363	7, 10, 14, 26, 64, 168, 320, 457, 477, 493, 511, 512, 513	67, 80, 87, 90, 120, 135, 170, 216, 254, 296, 333, 336, 339, 343, 344, 440, 486, 493, 516, 546, 604, 656, 687, 718, 792, 881, 891, 918, 948, 1016, 1050, 1088, 1185	35, 69, 129, 168, 179, 202, 257, 306, 330, 708, 711, 748, 908, 980, 1022, 1079, 1110, 1177, 1234, 1236, 1249, 1250, 1271, 1275, 1278
TOTAL:	13	13	33	25
Fetters Cut	47, 59, 62, 76, 86, 91, 111, 142, 188, 195, 203, 235, 334, 364, 396,	4, 12, 166, 167, 337, 350, 351, 359, 360, 510	38, 73, 122, 135, 136, 138, 176, 181, 382, 196, 254, 290, 298, 380, 458, 605, 657, 793, 865, 892, 1125, 1184, 1186	14, 15, 142, 162, 195, 282, 306, 400, 413, 414, 417, 457, 519, 521, 633, 640, 644, 671, 680, 691, 699, 707, 750, 1014, 1021, 1022, 1105, 1019, 1165, 1177, 1184, 1234, 1242, 1277
TOTAL:	15	10	23	34

	Therīgāthā		Theragāthā	
Technical Term	Author	Other	Author	Other
Nibbāna	15, 16, 18, 21, 34, 45, 46, 53, 66, 76, 86, 101, 105, 132, 222, 450, 517	6, 359, 432, 476, 477, 521	5, 7, 8, 79, 96, 298, 725, 948, 1047, 1060	32, 71, 100, 138, 162, 210, 227, 263, 364, 369, 392, 415, 418, 576, 586, 637, 658, 672, 702, 704, 725, 807, 809, 811, 813, 815, 817, 905, 906, 919, 928, 990, 1015, 1017, 1022, 1045, 1046, 1090, 1122, 1158, 1065, 1212. 1218, 1230, 1238, 1263, 1266, 1274
TOTAL:	17	6	10	48
Triple Knowl-edge Obtained	26, 30, 65, 121, 126, 150, 180, 181, 187, 194, 202, 331, 363, 433,	209, 251, 290, 311, 322, 323, 324	24, 55, 66, 107, 108, 112, 117, 220, 221, 224, 270, 274, 286, 296, 302, 314, 319, 336, 349, 410, 465, 479, 515, 562, 639, 886, 903, 1262	60, 129, 1114, 1177, 1236, 1248, 1249
TOTAL	13	7	28	7

Appendix A: Technical Terms for Liberation

	Therīgāthā		Theragāthā	
Technical Term	Author	Other	Author	Other
Freedom Obtained	11, 17, 30, 81, 96, 105, 111, 116, 144, 157, 223, 334, 369, 399	2, 320, 350, 506, 515	1, 43, 89, 181, 182, 253, 270, 274, 302, 319, 365, 410, 465, 477, 493, 516, 658, 996, 1017	47, 60, 438, 545, 596, 641, 642, 680, 691, 711, 906, 961, 1013, 1165, 1176, 1202, 1250, 1264, 1274
TOTAL:	14	5	19	19
Āsavas Destroyed	66, 71, 76, 99, 101, 121, 126, 181, 228, 334, 336, 364, 389	4, 205, 209, 329, 337	47, 116, 120, 122, 161, 198, 206, 218, 296, 333, 336, 337, 365, 439, 458, 546, 629, 791, 890, 896, 897, 996, 1061, 1179	92, 100, 129, 162, 178, 205, 289, 364, 369, 437, 438, 526, 541, 543, 576, 586, 596, 636, 672, 704, 711, 840, 900, 924, 928, 1022
TOTAL:	13	5	24	26

	Therīgāthā		Theragāthā	
Technical Term	Author	Other	Author	Other
Buddha's Teaching Done	26, 30, 36, 38, 41, 71, 96, 187, 194, 202, 228, 233, 331	13, 209, 311	24, 55, 66, 107, 108, 112, 117, 135, 220, 224, 270, 274, 286, 302, 314, 319, 332, 349, 410, 465, 515, 562, 604, 639, 656, 687, 792, 886, 891, 903, 918, 1016, 1050, 1088, 1185, 1260	746, 1114
TOTAL:	13	3	36	2
Pain Gone	52, 53, 131, 138, 144,	162, 167, 193, 206, 214, 281, 315, 318, 319, 512	78, 120, 339, 440	68, 82, 84, 138, 195, 227, 257, 263, 421, 492, 502, 503, 504, 505, 506, 519, 521, 525, 526, 585, 676, 677, 678, 682, 707, 712, 717, 721, 723, 1008, 1115, 1116, 1123, 1221, 1230
TOTAL:	5	10	4	35

Appendix A: Technical Terms for Liberation

	Therīgāthā		Theragāthā	
Technical Term	**Author**	**Other**	**Author**	**Other**
Darkness Torn Asunder	28, 44, 59, 62, 120, 142, 173, 174, 180, 188, 195, 203, 235	3	128, 170, 627	
TOTAL:	13	1	3	0
Peace Obtained	18, 86, 91, 182, 189, 369	14, 20, 168, 196, 212	50, 79, 260, 298, 325, 326, 416, 427, 434, 791	11, 32, 68, 239, 364, 369, 405, 422, 438, 521, 642, 672, 690, 747, 876, 905, 988, 1006, 1007, 1008, 1077, 1099, 1168, 1169, 1218, 1222, 1226
TOTAL:	6	5	10	27
Conquest	7, 10, 56, 59, 62, 65, 142, 188, 195, 203, 235		5, 6, 7, 8, 336	7, 177, 236, 415, 831, 833, 839, 1095, 1096, 1146, 1147, 1148, 1149, 1166, 1221, 1242
TOTAL:	11	0	5	16

	Therīgāthā		Theragāthā	
Technical Term	**Author**	**Other**	**Author**	**Other**
Rest Obtained	223	6, 8, 9, 211	604, 656, 687, 792, 891, 918, 1016, 1050, 1088, 1185	32, 69, 227, 263, 415, 990, 1021
TOTAL:	1	4	10	7
Fear Overcome	32	135, 333, 512,	5, 7, 20, 21, 189, 190, 709, 864, 1059	7, 82, 289, 367, 413, 707, 708, 716, 732, 831, 840, 912, 1093, 1238
TOTAL:	1	3	9	14
Far Shore Reached		291, 320	38, 632	66, 209, 680, 690, 711, 748, 763, 771, 772, 773, 1022, 1171, 1182, 1249, 1251, 1253, 1254
TOTAL:	0	2	2	17

APPENDIX B

Tables of Liberated *Therīs* and *Theras*

The following tables consist of a list of *therīs* and *theras* who are described (by themselves or by others), in the past or present tense, with the technical terms for liberation identified in Appendix A. These ascribed authors I refer to as 'liberated', though all the *therīs* and *theras* are attributed by the commentary with having attained liberation. In the tables, I simply indicate the terms or phrases that are used in their poems to describe the ascribed author, though, in many cases, the terms or phrases may be used repeatedly for a particular *therī* or *thera*. To determine if a particular term or phrase is used repeatedly, refer to the verse numbers of the *therī* or *thera* in question under the term or phrase in the table in Appendix A.

THERĪGĀTHĀ	
Author	**Technical Term**
Unknown Bhikkhunī (1)	Desire Overcome
Another Dhira (7)	Conquest
Upasamā (10)	Conquest
Muttā (11)	Rebirth Ended, Freedom Obtained
Uttarā (15)	*Nibbāna*, Desire Overcome
Sumanā (16)	*Nibbāna*, Desire Overcome
Dhammā (17)	Freedom Obtained
Sanghā (18)	*Nibbāna*, Desire Overcome, Peace Obtained
Jentī (21–22)	*Nibbāna*
Unknown Bhikkhunī (23–24)	Desire Overcome
Aḍḍhakāsī (25–26)	Rebirth Ended, Triple Knowledge Obtained, Buddha's Teaching Done
Cittā (27–28)	Darkness Torn Asunder

THERĪGĀTHĀ	
Author	**Technical Term**
Mettikā (29–30)	Darkness Torn Asunder, Freedom Obtained, Buddha's Teaching Done
Mittā (31–32)	Fear Overcome
Abhayamāt (33–34)	*Nibbāna*, Desire Overcome
Abhayattheī (35–36)	Desire Overcome, Buddha's Teaching Done
Sāmā (37–38)	Desire Overcome, Buddha's Teaching Done
Another Sāmā (39–41)	Desire Overcome, Buddha's Teaching Done
Uttamā (42–44)	Desire Overcome, Darkness Torn Asunder
Another Uttamā (45–47)	*Nibbāna*, Rebirth Ended, Fetters Cut
Ubbirī (51–53)	*Nibbāna*, Desire Overcome, Pain Gone
Sukkā (54–56)	Desire Overcome, Rebirth Ended, Conquest
Selā (57–59)	Fetters Cut, Darkness Torn Asunder, Conquest
Somā (60–62)	Fetters Cut, Darkness Torn Asunder, Conquest

THERĪGĀTHĀ	
Author	**Technical Term**
Bhaddā Kapilānī (63–66)	*Nibbāna*, Rebirth Ended, *Āsavas* Destroyed, Conquest, Triple Knowledge Obtained
Unknown Bhikkhunī (67–71)	*Āsavas* Destroyed, Buddha's Teaching Done
Vimalā (72–76)	*Nibbāna*, Fetters Cut, *Asavas* Destroyed
Sīhā (77–81)	Freedom Obtained
Nandā (82–86)	*Nibbāna*, Fetters Cut, Peace Obtained
Nanduttarā (87–91)	Desire Overcome, Rebirth Ended, Fetters Cut, Peace Obtained
Mittakālī (92–96)	Freedom Obtained, Buddha's Teaching Done
Sakulā (97–101)	*Nibbāna*, Desire Overcome, *Āsavas* Destroyed
Soṇā (102-106)	*Nibbāna*, Desire Overcome, Rebirth Ended, Freedom Obtained
Bhaddā (107–111)	Fetters Cut, Freedom Obtained
Paṭācārā (112-116)	Freedom Obtained
Thirty Bhikkhunīs (117–121)	*Āsavas* Destroyed, Darkness Torn Asunder, Triple Knowledge Obtained

THERĪGĀTHĀ	
Author	**Technical Term**
Candā (122–126)	*Āsavas* Destroyed, Triple Knowledge Obtained
Pañcasatā Paṭācārā (127–132)	*Nibbāna*, Desire Overcome, Pain Gone
Vāsiṭṭhī (133–138)	Pain Gone
Khemā (139–144)	Desire Overcome, Fetters Cut, Pain Gone, Darkness Torn Asunder, Conquest, Freedom Obtained
Sujātā (145–150)	Rebirth Ended, Triple Knowledge Obtained
Anopamā (151–156)	Desire Overcome, Freedom Obtained
Mahāpajāpatī Gotamī (157-162)	Desire Overcome, Rebirth Ended
Vijayā (169–174)	Darkness Torn Asunder
Uttarā (175–181)	*Āsavas* Destroyed, Darkness Torn Asunder, Triple Knowledge Obtained
Cālā (182–188)	Fetters Cut, Darkness Torn Asunder, Conquest, Triple Knowledge Obtained, Buddha's Teaching Done, Peace Obtained
Upacālā (189-195)	Fetters Cut, Darkness Torn Asunder, Conquest, Triple Knowledge Obtained, Buddha's Teaching Done, Peace Obtained

THERĪGĀTHĀ	
Author	**Technical Term**
Sīsūpacālā (196–203)	Fetters Cut, Darkness Torn Asunder, Conquest, Triple Knowledge Obtained, Buddha's Teaching Done
Vaḍḍhamātā (204–212)	Desire Overcome
Kisāgotamī (213–223)	*Nibbāna*, Rebirth Ended, Freedom Obtained, Rest Obtained
Uppalavaṇṇā (224–235)	Fetters Cut, *Āsavas* Destroyed, Darkness Torn Asunder, Conquest, Buddha's Teaching Done
Sundarī (312–337)	Desire Overcome, Rebirth Ended, Fetters Cut, *Āsavas* Destroyed, Triple Knowledge Obtained, Freedom Obtained, Buddha's Teaching Done
Subhā Jīvakamba-vanikā (366–399)	Desire Overcome, Fetters Cut, *Āsavas* Destroyed, Freedom Obtained
Isidāsī (400–447)	Triple Knowledge Obtained
Sumedhā (448–522)	*Nibbāna*

THERĪGĀTHĀ	
Author	**Technical Term**
Subhūti (1)	Freedom Obtained
Dabba (5)	*Nibbāna*, Conquest, Fear Overcome
Sītavaniya (6)	Conquest
Balliya (7)	*Nibbāna*, Conquest, Fear Overcome
Vīra (8)	*Nibbāna*, Conquest
Ajita (20)	Desire Overcome, Fear Overcome
Nigrodha (21)	Fear Overcome
Sugandha (24)	Triple Knowledge Obtained, Buddha's Teaching Done
Gavampati (39)	Fetters Cut, Far Shore Reached
Sumaṅgala (43)	Freedom Obtained
Ujjaya (47)	*Āsavas* Destroyed
Vimala (50)	Peace Obtained
Añjanāvaniya (55)	Triple Knowledge Obtained, Buddha's Teaching Done

THERĪGĀTHĀ	
Author	**Technical Term**
Kuṭivihārī (56)	Desire Overcome
Meghiya (66)	Triple Knowledge Obtained, Buddha's Teaching Done
Ekadhamma-savanīya (67)	Rebirth Ended
Māṇava (73)	Fetters Cut
Meṇḍasira (78)	Pain Gone
Rakkhita (79)	*Nibbāna*, Desire Overcome, Peace Obtained
Ugga (80)	Rebirth Ended
Paviṭṭha (87)	Rebirth Ended
Devasabha (89)	Freedom Obtained
Sāmidatta (90)	Rebirth Ended
Khaṇḍasumana (96)	*Nibbāna*
Dhammasava (107)	Triple Knowledge Obtained, Buddha's Teaching Done

THERĪGĀTHĀ	
Author	**Technical Term**
Dhammasava-pitā (108)	Triple Knowledge Obtained, Buddha's Teaching Done
Vacchagotta (112)	Triple Knowledge Obtained, Buddha's Teaching Done
Pārāpariya (116)	*Āsavas* Destroyed
Yasa (117)	Triple Knowledge Obtained, Buddha's Teaching Done
Isidatta (120)	Rebirth Ended, *Āsavas* Destroyed, Pain Gone
Uttara (121–122)	Fetters Cut, *Āsavas* Destroyed
Gaṅgātīriya (127–128)	Darkness Torn Asunder
Surādha (135-136)	Rebirth Ended, Fetters Cut, Buddha's Teaching Done
Gotama (137–138)	Fetters Cut
Nanda (157–158)	Desire Overcome
Uttara (161–162)	Desire Overcome, *Āsavas* Destroyed
Vītasoka (169–170)	Rebirth Ended, Darkness Torn Asunder
Bharata (175–176)	Fetters Cut

THERĪGĀTHĀ	
Author	**Technical Term**
Kaṇhadinna (179–180)	Desire Overcome
Migasira (181–182)	Fetters Cut, Freedom Obtained
Sambulakaccāna (189–190)	Fear Overcome
Khitaka (191–192)	Desire Overcome
Nisabha (195–196)	Fetters Cut
Usabha (197–198)	*Āsavas* Destroyed
Brahmāli (205–206)	*Āsavas* Destroyed
Vajjita (215–216)	Rebirth Ended
Sandhita (217–218)	*Āsavas* Destroyed
Aṅgaṇika-bhāradvāja (219–221)	Triple Knowledge Obtained, Buddha's Teaching Done
Paccaya (222–224)	Triple Knowledge Obtained, Buddha's Teaching Done
Uttarapāla (252–254)	Rebirth Ended, Fetters Cut, Freedom Obtained
Gotama (258–260)	Peace Obtained

THERĪGĀTHĀ	
Author	**Technical Term**
Nāgasamāla (267–270)	Triple Knowledge Obtained, Freedom Obtained, Buddha's Teaching Done
Bhagu (271–274)	Triple Knowledge Obtained, Freedom Obtained, Buddha's Teaching Done
Jambuka (283–286)	Triple Knowledge Obtained, Buddha's Teaching Done
Senaka (287–290)	Fetters Cut
Rāhula (295–298)	*Nibbāna*, Desire Overcome, Rebirth Ended, Fetters Cut, *Āsavas* Destroyed, Triple Knowledge Obtained, Peace Obtained
Candana (299–302)	Triple Knowledge Obtained, Freedom Obtained, Buddha's Teaching Done
Mudita (311–314)	Triple Knowledge Obtained, Buddha's Teaching Done
Rājadatta (315–319)	Triple Knowledge Obtained, Freedom Obtained, Buddha's Teaching Done
Girimānanda (325–329)	Desire Overcome, Triple Knowledge Obtained, Peace Obtained
Sumana (330–334)	Rebirth Ended, *Āsavas* Destroyed, Buddha's Teaching Done
Vaḍḍha (335–339)	Desire Overcome, Rebirth Ended, *Āsavas* Destroyed, Pain Gone, Conquest, Triple Knowledge Obtained
Nadīkassapa (340–344)	Desire Overcome, Rebirth Ended

THERĪGĀTHĀ	
Author	**Technical Term**
Gayākassapa (345–349)	Triple Knowledge Obtained, Buddha's Teaching Done
Soṇa Kuṭikaṇṇa (365–369)	*Āsavas* Destroyed, Freedom Obtained
Uruveḷakassapa (375–380)	Desire Overcome, Fetters Cut,
Sappadāsa (405–410)	Triple Knowledge Obtained, Freedom Obtained, Buddha's Teaching Done
Kātiyāna (411–416)	Desire Overcome, Peace Obtained
Jenta Purohitaputta (423–428)	Peace Obtained
Sumana (429–434)	Peace Obtained
Nhātakamuni (435–440)	Rebirth Ended, *Āsavas* Destroyed, Pain Gone
Sabbakāma (453–458)	Fetters Cut, *Āsavas* Destroyed
Sundara-samudda (459–465)	Triple Knowledge Obtained, Freedom Obtained, Buddha's Teaching Done
Lakuṇṭaka (466–472)	Desire Overcome
Bhadda (473–479)	Triple Knowledge Obtained, Freedom Obtained

THERĪGĀTHĀ	
Author	**Technical Term**
Sopāka (480-486)	Rebirth Ended
Sarabhaṅga (487-493)	Rebirth Ended, Freedom Obtained
Mahāpanthaka (510-517)	Desire Overcome, Rebirth Ended, Triple Knowledge Obtained, Freedom Obtained, Buddha's Teaching Done
Ekavihāriya (537-546)	Rebirth Ended, *Āsavas* Destroyed
Cūḷapanthaka (557-566)	Triple Knowledge Obtained, Buddha's Teaching Done
Sakicca (597-607)	Rebirth Ended, Fetters Cut, Buddha's Teaching Done, Rest Obtained
Sunīta (620-631)	*Āsavas* Destroyed, Darkness Ṭorn Asunder
Soṇa Koḷivisa (632-644)	Triple Knowledge Obtained, Buddha's Teaching Done, Far Shore Reached
Revata (645-658)	Rebirth Ended, Fetters Cut, Freedom Obtained, Buddha's Teaching Done, Rest Obtained
Aññākoṇḍañña (673-688)	Rebirth Ended, Buddha's Teaching Done, Rest Obtained
Adhimutta (705-725)	*Nibbāna*, Rebirth Ended, Fear Overcome
Raṭṭhapāla (769-793)	Rebirth Ended, Fetters Cut, *Āsavas* Destroyed, Buddha's Teaching Done, Peace Obtained, Rest Obtained

THERĪGĀTHĀ	
Author	**Technical Term**
Bhaddiya (842–865)	Desire Overcome, Fetters Cut, Fear Overcome
Aṅgulimāla (866–891)	Desire Overcome, Rebirth Ended, *Āsavas* Destroyed, Triple Knowledge Obtained, Buddha's Teaching Done, Rest Obtained
Anuruddha (892–919)	Rebirth Ended, Fetters Cut, *Āsavas* Destroyed, Triple Knowledge Obtained, Buddha's Teaching Done, Rest Obtained
Pārāpariya (920–948)	*Nibbāna*, Rebirth Ended
Sāriputta (981–1017)	Rebirth Ended, *Āsavas* Destroyed, Freedom Obtained, Buddha's Teaching Done, Rest Obtained
Ānanda (1018–1050)	*Nibbāna*, Rebirth Ended, Buddha's Teaching Done, Rest Obtained
Mahākassapa (1051–1090)	*Nibbāna*, Desire Overcome, Rebirth Ended, *Āsavas* Destroyed, Fear Overcome, Buddha's Teaching Done, Rest Obtained
Tālapuṭa (1091–1145)	Desire Overcome, Fetters Cut
Mahā-moggallāna (1146–1208)	Rebirth Ended, Fetters Cut, *Āsavas* Destroyed, Buddha's Teaching Done, Rest Obtained
Vaṅgīsa (1209–1279)	Triple Knowledge Obtained, Buddha's Teaching Done

APPENDIX C

Images of the Environment

The following table contains every reference to the most commonly used images of the environment used in the *Therīgāthā* and *Thergāthā*.

In the table, I distinguish between images used as settings and those used as symbols. The 'setting' category includes images that describe the actual setting of any of the characters in the texts, the ascribed authors, others who appear in their poems, or examples they discuss. The 'symbol' category includes images used as metaphors, similes, or analogies. In any case where this distinction is unclear, I define the image as 'setting'. For discussion of this distinction, see pp. 86–89.

I also evaluate whether a particular image is used positively (+), negatively (–), or ambivalently (*). My criteria for evaluation is whether or not the image is presented as conducive to, or expressive of, liberation, meditation, or exemplary figures (+), inconducive to liberation, meditation, or expressive of the situation or attitude of non-Buddhists (–), or ambivalent with regards to liberation, meditation, or Buddhist doctrine (*). My findings are condensed in Table 3, 'Images of the Surroundings,' and are discussed at length in Chapter IV.

	Therīgāthā		Thergāthā	
Image	Setting	Symbol	Setting	Symbol
Forest or Trees Darkness	+24, +50, *51, +75, −80, +81, −143, +147, −230, +362, −366, −370, −371, −372, −373, −375	*254, *263, *267, −297, −394, −478, −490	+6, +18, +31, +55, +59, +62, +110, −115, +119, +155, +217, −219, +309, −350, +351, +352, +353, +354, −435, +436, +466, +467, +524, +527, +528, +537, +538, +539, +540, +541, +542, +543, +544, +545, +563, +592, +597, +602, +626, +684 *688, +832, +851, +852, +864, +868, −887, +919, +920, +925, +948, +962, +991, +992, +998, +1092, +1102, +1108, +1113, +1120, +1135, +1136, +1137, +1144, +1146, +1147, +1148, +1149, +1208	−2, +14, *62, +64, −72, −109, +110, −342, −399, −691, −762, −788, −1006, −1007, +1121, +1202
TOTAL:	+6 −9 *1 — 16	+0 −4 *3 — 7	+63 −5 *1 — 69	+6 −10 *1 — 17

Appendix C: Images of the Environment

	Therīgāthā		Thergāthā	
Image	**Setting**	**Symbol**	**Setting**	**Symbol**
Mountain or Rock or Cave	+27, +28, +29, +30, +48, +108	−297, −381, −384, −497	+13, +23, +41, +110, +113, −115, +309, +524, +525, +540, +544, +545, +601, +602, −887, +925, +1058, +1059, +1060, +1061, +1062, +1063, +1064, +1065, +1068, +1069, +1070, +1091, +1097, +1103, +1108, +1135, +1137, +1144, +1167, +1249	+177, +191, +192, +367, +643, +651, −680, −691, *692, +1000, *1013, −1133, +1202
TOTAL:	+6 −0 *0 — 6	+0 −4 *0 — 4	+33 −2 *0 — 35	+8 −3 *2 — 13

	Therīgāthā		Thergāthā	
Image	**Setting**	**Symbol**	**Setting**	**Symbol**
Wild Animals and Insects	–303, –373, –436, –437	–23, –241, *252, *261, +299, +332, –353, –398, –451, –467, –475, –488, –500, –502, –508	+13, +22, –31, +49, +113, +211, +244, +307, +308, +310, –393, +522, +524, +577, +599, +601, +602, +684, +1063, +1065, +1068, +1069, +1070, +1097, +1103, +1108, +1113, +1135, +1136	+92, –109, –125, –126, –151, +175, +177, +229, –297, –362, +367, –387, +390, –399, –429, –454, –457, –576, –749, +774, +775, +832, +840, –989, +1036, –1080, +1081, +1095, –1111, –1128, +1144, –1154, –1175, +1232, +1270
TOTAL:	+0 –4 *0 — 4	+2 –11 *2 — 15	+27 –2 *0 — 29	+16 –19 *0 — 35
Tame Animals	–325, –326, –327, –328, –438, –439, –440	+114, +229, –509		+16, –17, +45, –101, +173, +174, +205, +206, +358, +433, –446, +476, +629, +659, –976, –1025, +1084, +1140, +1179
TOTAL:	+0 –7 *0 — 7	+2 –1 *0 — 3	+0 –0 *0 — 0	+14 –5 *0 — 19

	Therīgāthā		Thergāthā	
Image	Setting	Symbol	Setting	Symbol
Elephants (Wild or Tame)	+48, +49, −327, −328, −373	−7, −10, −56, −65, *267, +301	*194, +197, +198, +539, −842, +1062, +1064	+31, +77, −177, +244, +256, +289, −355, −356, −357, +684, +692, +693, +694, +695, +696, +697, +698, +699, +703, +704, +967, +968, +1105, −1130, −1139, −1141, +1147, +1149, −1166, +1184, +1240, +1279
TOTAL:	+2 −3 *0 — 5	+1 −4 *1 — 6	+5 −1 *1 — 7	+24 −8 *0 — 32
Rain or Rainy Season		+55, −487	+1, +24, +41; +50, +51, +52, +53, +54, +110, +128, +189, +211, +325, +326, +327, +328, +329, +522, +524, *531, *597, +1065, +1102, +1108, +1135, +1136, +1137, *1153, +1167	−133, −134, −400, *447, −598, +675, *985, +1240, +1273
TOTAL:	+0 −0 *0 — 0	+1 −1 *0 — 2	+26 −0 *3 — 29	+3 −4 *2 — 9

	Therīgāthā		Thergāthā	
Image	**Setting**	**Symbol**	**Setting**	**Symbol**
Flowing Water	−87, +114, −236, −237, +306,+309	+12, −239, −243, −497, −500	+13, +113, +287, +307, +308, +309, +310, +340, −345, +430, −523, +601, +1063, +1070, *1190	*38, −145, −147, +168, −265, +349, −402, −412, +415, *556, +660, −761, −762, −777, *1013, *1104, −1133
TOTAL:	+3 −3 *0 — 6	+1 −4 *0 — 5	+13 −1 *1 — 15	+4 −9 *4 — 17
Stagnant Water (Flood or Bog)		−291, −354		+7, −15, −88, −89, −124, −285, −495, −567, −572, −633, −680, −681, −700, −759, −880, −894, −1053, −1131, −1154
TOTAL:	+0 −0 *0 — 0	+0 −2 *0 — 2	+0 −0 *0 — 0	+1 −18 *0 — 19

	Therīgāthā		Thergāthā	
Image	Setting	Symbol	Setting	Symbol
Darkness or Night	+120, +172, +173, +179, +180, +322, +323, +324	−3, −28, −44, −59, −62, −120, −142, −173, −174, −180, −188, −195, −203, −235	−84, *145, +165, +193, −207, −231, +366, −385, +517, +524, +627	−128, −170, −292, −361, *397, −451, −452, −627, −1034, −1048, −1268
TOTAL:	+8 −0 *0 — 8	+0 −14 *0 — 14	+6 −4 *1 — 11	+0 −10 *1 — 11
Light (Moon, Fire, Lamp, Sun)	+115, −143	+2, +3, −87, −116, −200, −384, −386, −398, −488, −493, −504, −507	−84, −219, +477	+3, +26, +158, +294, +306, +343, −415, −416, +417, +426, +546, +548, −702, −790, +820, +871, +872, +873, −906, +1014, +1023, +1026, −1099, +1119, +1156, +1204, +1205, +1212, +1237, +1244, +1252, +1258, +1269
TOTAL:	+1 −1 *0 — 2	+2 −10 *0 — 12	+1 −2 *0 — 3	+27 −6 *0 — 33

	Therīgāthā		Thergāthā	
Image	**Setting**	**Symbol**	**Setting**	**Symbol**
Hut			+1, +51, +52, +53, +54, +55, +56, +58, +59, +60, +127, +325, +326, +327, +328, +329, *487	−57, *125, −133, +134, −256, −1147, −1149, −1150
TOTAL:	+0 −0 *0 — 0	+0 −0 *0 — 0	+16 −0 *1 — 17	+1 −6 *1 — 8
Vihāra or Cell	−37, −42, −68, +94, +115, +147, −169, +518		+222, +223, +224, −271, +272, +313, +385, −406, +408, +477, +480	
TOTAL:	+4 −4 *0 — 8	+0 −0 *0 — 0	+9 −2 *0 — 11	+0 −0 *0 — 0

	Therīgāthā		Thergātha	
Image	**Setting**	**Symbol**	**Setting**	**Symbol**
House or Palace	–73, +97, –146, *218, –376, *410, *414, *421, *425, +427, +428, +461, +480, +494	–18, –92, *270, +389	–34, +208, +234, +235, +847, –1107	–48, –107, –111, –136, –183, –184, +193, –645, –688, –712, –786, *1190, *1192, *1194, *1196, *1198, –1209
TOTAL:	+6 –3 *5 — 14	+1 –2 *1 — 4	+4 –2 *0 — 6	+1 –6 *1 — 17
Village or City	+135, +282, –294, –304,	–305, +317, +319, –340, +400, *405, *435, +448	+14, +23, *34, +197, +622, –863, +919, –946, –962, +991, *1054, –1253	–245, +653, +1005
TOTAL:	+6 –4 *2 — 12	+0 –0 *0 — 0	+6 –4 *2 — 12	+2 –1 *0 — 3

APPENDIX D

Settings of Liberated *Therīs* and *Theras*

The following two tables present liberated *therīs* or *theras* (see Appendix A) for whom a setting is provided, either during their liberation experience, or subsequent to it. Table 1, 'Settings of Liberated Authors', is categorized by the most common images used in the *Therīgāthā* and *Theragāthā* (see Appendix C), cited by the first verse of each poem, though many of the poems use the same image repeatedly. To determine if a particular *therī* or *thera* uses the image repeatedly, refer to the verse numbers that comprise her or his poems (Appendix B) and consult the references of the image (Appendix C).

Table 2, 'Liberated Authors Who Provide a Setting', consists of a list of the liberated *therīs* and *theras* who are situated in a setting. The calculation at the bottom of the table refers to the percentage of liberated authors who provide a setting in comparison with the total number of liberated authors in each text (see Appendix B). The references in this table are cited by the first verse of each poem.

Table 1

Settings of Liberated Authors

SETTING	THERĪS	THERAS
Forest	23, 51, 72, 77, 145, 224, 338, 366	6, 55, 217, 435, 466, 537, 557, 597, 620, 842, 866, 892, 920, 1051, 1146
Mountain	27, 29, 107	537, 597, 866, 1051, 1091
Wild Animals		597, 1051, 1091
Tame Animals		
Elephants		197, 537, 1051
Rain		1, 24, 50, 127, 325, 597, 1051, 1091
River	112	287, 429, 1051
Flood		
Dark	117, 169, 175	510
Light	112, 139	473
Hut		1, 55, 56, 127, 325
Vihāra	37, 42, 67 ,92, 112, 145, 169	222, 271, 311, 405, 473, 480
House	72, 97, 145, 400, 448	842, 1091
City	133, 400, 448	197, 620, 892, 1051

Table 2

Liberated Authors Who Provide a Setting

Therīgāthā	23, 27, 29, 37, 42, 51, 67, 72, 77, 92, 97, 107, 112, 117, 133, 139, 145, 169, 175, 224, 338, 366, 400, 448 TOTAL: 24 of 56 or 42.9%
Theragāthā	1, 6, 24, 50, 55, 56, 127, 197, 217, 222, 271, 287, 311, 325, 405, 429, 435, 466, 473, 480, 510, 537, 557, 597, 620, 842, 866, 892, 920, 1051, 1091, 1146 TOTAL: 32 of 97 or 33%

NOTES

Introduction: The *Therīgāthā:* Text and Context

1. C.A.F. Rhys Davids (trans.), *Psalms of the Sisters* (London: Luzac and Co. Ltd., 1909 [reprint, 1964]), p. 8; cited hereafter as *Sisters*.
2. Other religious textual traditions contain texts that claim female authorship, but none, to my knowledge, that are part of the 'canon', i.e., the corpus of literature defined as scripture in a select council at an early point in the religion's history who assumed responsibility for defining and delimiting inspirational literature. The *Acts of Thecla* in the Christian apocryphal tradition is a case in point; see Edgar Hennecke and W. Schneemelcher (ed. and trans.), *New Testament Apocrypha* (Philadelphia: Westminster Press, 1965), pp. 322–364. Though the text originated in an early period of Christian history, and though it was accepted as canonical for centuries, it was ultimately excluded from the canon. For a study of this fascinating text and arguments for its female authorship, see Dennis MacDonald, *The Legend and the Apostle: the Battle for Paul in Story and Canon* (Philadelphia: Westminster Press, 1983).
3. Most recent studies of women in Buddhism have included a discussion of the *Therīgāthā*. See for example, Rita Gross, *Buddhism After Patriarchy* (Albany: State University of New York Press, 1993), especially, pp. 48–54, Kevin Trainor, 'In the Eye of the Beholder: Nonattachment and the Body in Subhā's Verse (*Therīgāthā* 71),' *Journal of the American Academy of Religion* 41 (1993): 57–79, Susan Murcott, *The First Buddhist Women: Translations and Commentary on the Therīgāthā* (Berkeley: Parallax Press, 1991), Karen Lang, 'Lord Death's Snare: Gender-Related Imagery in the *Theragāthā* and the *Therīgāthā*,' *Journal of Feminist Studies in Religion* 2 (1986):

63–79, and Nancy Schuster Barnes, 'Buddhism,' in Arvind Sharma (ed.), *Women in World Religions* (Albany: State University of New York Press, 1987), pp. 105–133.

4. Richard Gombrich, 'Feminine Elements in Sinhalese Buddhism,' *Wiener Zeitschrift für die Kunde Südasiens und Archiv fur Indische Philosophie* 14–16 (1970–72): 67–93. I have yet to view this film, though I am certainly interested in doing so.
5. Personal communication with Swarna Gunasekera. Again, I have not heard this song, but I am very intrigued by the prospect of a popular song about Subhā.
6. K.R. Norman, *Elders' Verses II* (London: Luzac and Co. Ltd., 1971), p. xxxi.
7. See for example, Alan Dundes, *Interpreting Folklore* (Bloomington: Indiana University Press, 1987), Albert Lord, *The Singer of Tales* (Cambridge: Harvard University Press, 1960), Richard Bauman, *Story, Performance and Event: Contextual Studies of Oral Narrative* (Cambridge: Cambridge University Press, 1986), and especially Elaine Lawless, 'Rescripting Their Lives and Narratives: Spiritual Life Stories of Pentacostal Women Preachers,' *Journal of Feminist Studies in Religion* 7 (1991): 53–72. Lawless's work is particularly interesting as she illustrates in fascinating detail how women in an overwhelmingly patriarchal environment employ similar, almost formulaic, life-stories to justify their unconventional decision to become public speakers.
8. The term 'poem' is used out of convenience to designate compilations of verses attributed to an author or group. No aesthetic or technical meaning is implied.
9. The numbers in parentheses refer to verse numbers. When a whole poem is implied, only the first verse number is cited.
10. K.R. Norman, *Elders' Verses Vol. I and II* (London, Luzac and Co. Ltd., 1969–1971), p. xx and p. xxvii; hereafter cited as *Theragāthā* and *Therīgāthā*, respectively.
11. See William Stede, 'The *Pādas* of the *Thera-* and *Therī-gāthā*,' *Journal of the Pali Text Society*, 1924–27, pp. 31–226; especially his table of repeated *pādas*, pp. 197–226.
12. *Theragāthā*, p. xxi.
13. A.K. Warder, *Pali Metre* (London: Luzac and Co. Ltd., 1967), p. 136. Warder bases this early dating of the poem on strophe length, level of complexity, and the linking of verses through verbal and rhythmic repetitions and patterns which, he claims, are techniques of Middle Indian lyric poetry (p. 137).
14. C.A.F. Rhys Davids, *Sisters*, p. 8. See the opening quote to this introduction.

15. Siegfried Lienhard, 'Sur la Structure Poetique des *Thera-Therīgāthā*,' *Journal Asiatique* 263 (1975): 375–396.
16. Throughout this study, I make a distinction between 'authors' and '*therīs* or *theras*'. By 'authors', I refer to the actual composers, recognizing that these authors may in fact have been the redactors or reciters who may have transformed the utterances they were attempting to preserve. '*Therīs* or *theras*' refer to ascribed authors, the names of whom are used for convenience, recognizing again, that these ascribed authors may not correspond with the actual composers.
17. Étienne Lamotte, *History of Indian Buddhism*, trans. Sara Webb-Boin (Louvain-La-Neuve: Peeters Press, 1988), p. 161, quoting the *Saṃyutta Nikāya I*, p. 209 and the *Divyāvadāna*, pp. 34–35.
18. *Aṅguttara Nikāya* I, chapter 14, sections 1–6.
19. Clifford Geertz, 'Religion as a Cultural System,' Chapter IV of *The Interpretation of Cultures* (New York: Basic Books, Inc., 1973), pp. 87–125.
20. George Lakoff and Mark Johnson, *Metaphors We Live By* (Chicago: University of Chicago Press, 1980).
21. Thanks to Graeme MacQueen for the term 'symbolic universe'.
22. Other scholars have employed a similar approach in the study of Pali literature. See Steven Collins, *Selfless Persons: Imagery and Thought in Theravāda Buddhism* (Cambridge: Cambridge University Press, 1982). For studies of imagery specific to the *Therīgāthā* and *Theragāthā*, see B.G. Gokhale, 'The Image-World of the *Thera-Therī-Gāthās*' in D.H. De A. Wijesekera (ed.), *Malalasekara Commemoration Volume* (Colombo: Kularatne and Co. Ltd., 1976), pp. 96–110, Karen Lang, 'Images of Women in Early Buddhism and Christian Gnosticism,' *Buddhist and Christian Studies* 2 (1982): 95–105, and C.A.F. Rhys Davids, 'The Love of Nature in Buddhist Poems,' *The Quest: A Quarterly Review* 1 (1910): 416–434.
23. K.R. Norman (trans.), *Elders' Verses*, Vol. I–II (London: Luzac and Co. Ltd., 1969–1971).
24. Hermann Oldenberg and Richard Pischel, eds. *Thera-Therī-Gāthā*, second edition with appendices by K.R. Norman and L. Alsdorf (London: Luzac and Co., 1966).
25. See for example, R. Jordan and S. Kalcik (eds.), *Women's Folklore, Women's Culture* (Philadelphia: University of Pennsylvania Press, 1985), Caroline Walker Bynum, et al, eds., *Gender and Religion: On the Complexity of Symbols* (Boston: Beacon Press, 1986), Kristin Wardetsky, 'The Structure and Interpretation of Fairy Tales Composed by Children,' *Journal of American*

Folklore 103 (1990): 157–176, Eleanor Zelliot, 'Buddhist Women of the Contemporary Maharashtrian Conversion Movement,' in José Cabezón (ed.), *Buddhism, Sexuality, and Gender* (Albany: State University of New York Press, 1992), pp. 91–107.

26. Caroline Walker Bynum, *Holy Feast and Holy Fast: The Religious Significance of Food to Medieval Women* (Berkeley: University of California Press, 1987), '"And Women His Humanity": Female Imagery in the Religious Writing of the Later Middle Ages,' in Bynum, *Gender and Religion: On the Complexity of Symbols*, pp. 257–288, and especially, 'Women's Stories, Women's Symbols,' in R. Moore and F. Reynolds (eds.), *Anthropology and the Study of Religion* (Chicago: Centre for the Scientific Study of Religion, 1984), pp. 105–125.
27. See the citations in n. 3 above, and Alan Sponberg, 'Attitudes toward Women and the Feminine in Early Buddhism,' in Cabezón, *Buddhism, Sexuality, and Gender*, pp. 3–36, Nancy Falk, 'An Image of Woman in Old Buddhist Literature: The Daughters of Māra,' in J. Plaskow and J. Arnold (eds.), *Women and Religion* (Missoula: Scholars Press, 1974), pp. 105–112, Nancy Falk, 'The Case of the Vanishing Nuns: The Fruits of Ambivalence in Ancient Indian Buddhism,' in N. Falk and R. Gross (eds.), *Unspoken Worlds: Women's Religious Lives in Non-Western Cultures*, (San Fransisco: Harper and Row, 1980), pp. 207–224, Diana Paul, *Women in Buddhism* (Berkeley: University of California Press, 1979), and I.B. Horner's classic, *Women Under Primitive Buddhism* (London: George Routledge, 1930).
28. A.L. Basham, *The Wonder that was India* (London: Sidgwick and Jackson, 1954), pp. 180–181.
29. *Cullavagga* X. See Chapter II below for more discussion.
30. Padmanabh Jaini, *Gender and Salvation: Jaina Debates on the Spiritual Liberation of Women* (Berkeley: University of California Press, 1991). For more discussion of the attitudes towards women in Jain literature, see Nalini Balbir, 'Women in Jainism,' in Arvind Sharma (ed.), *Religion and Women* (Albany: State University of New York Press, 1994), pp. 121–138.

Chapter I: The Langauge of Liberation

1. An adapted translation by C.A.F. Rhys Davids, *Psalms of the Brethren* (London: Luzac and Co. Ltd., 1909 [reprint, 1964]), p. 3; cited hereafter as *Brethren.*
2. Gregory Schopen has recently challenged this assumption common to almost all studies of early Buddhist textual sources.

In his study of inscriptions at Amarāvatī, Schopen discovered no epigraphs which refer to the religious achievements of the monks. Furthermore, references to *arhats* do not appear until 6th or 7th century inscriptions. He takes this lacuna as evidence for his contention that Buddhist textual sources do not accurately reflect the ideas common among the religious communities. See 'An Old Inscription from Amarāvatī and the Cult of the Local Monastic Dead in Indian Buddhist Monasteries,' *Journal for the International Association of Buddhist Studies* 14 (1991): 99–137.

3. See Stede, 'The *Pādas* of the *Thera-* and *Therī-gāthā*,' pp. 31–226, Willem Bollée (ed.), *Reverse Index of the Dhammapada, Suttanipāta, Thera- and Therīgāthā Pādas* (Reinbek: Berlag fur Orientalistische Fachpublikationen, 1983), and Hajime Nakamura, 'Common Elements in Early Jain and Buddhist Literature,' *Indologica Taurinensia* 11 (1981): 303–330.
4. See, for example, I.B. Horner, *The Early Buddhist Theory of Man Perfected* (Amsterdam: Pilo Press, 1936 [reprint, 1975]), Guy Welbon, *The Buddhist Nirvāṇa and its Western Interpreters* (Chicago: University of Chicago Press, 1968), and especially Rune Johansson, *The Psychology of Nirvāṇa* (London: George Allen and Unwin Ltd., 1969) which refers very frequently to the *Therīgāthā* and the *Theragāthā*.
5. Norman, *Elders' Verses I*, p. xxix. For a general discussion of the orality of Pali texts, see Steven Collins, 'Notes on Some Oral Aspects of Pali Literature,' *Indo-Iranian Journal* 35 (1992): 121–135 and references therein.
6. Albert Lord, *The Singer of Tales* (Cambridge, Massachusetts: Harvard University Press, 1960).
7. See for example Ruth Finnegan 'What is Oral Literature Anyway? Comments in the Light of Some African and Other Comparative Material,' in Benjamin Stolz and Richard Shannon (eds.), *Oral Literature and the Formula* (Ann Arbor: University of Michigan, 1976), pp. 127–166, or Bruce Rosenberg, 'Oral Sermons and Oral Narrative,' in Dan Ben-Amos and Kenneth Goldstein (eds.), *Folklore: Performance and Communication* (The Hague: Mouton, 1975), pp. 75–101.
8. Lord, *Singer of Tales*, pp. 33–36.
9. *Ibid*, pp. 41–43.
10. As Lienhard has demonstrated, many of the poems also follow an established poetic tradition in ancient India; see 'Sur la Structure Poetique des *Thera-Therīgāthā*.'
11. The three knowledges are: (1) remembrance of former births, (2) insight into the destiny of all beings, and (3) recognition of the

origin of misery and of the way to its removal. *The Pali Text Society's Pali-English Dictionary* (hereafter, *PED*), 'te', p. 306.

12. I follow Norman's hesitation in translating the term '*āsavas*'. As he points out, the term has been translated as 'canker', 'passions', 'intoxicants', 'cravings', sin or sinful inclinations', and as 'influx of karman' (*Elders' Verses I*, n. 47, p. 134–5). The *PED* translates it as 'that which flows', and identifies it as referring to intoxicants and discharges, understood in terms of psychology as the intoxicating ideas of sesuality, lust for life, speculation, and ignorance that obstruct one's concentration on liberation.
13. The commentary identifies this narrator as the Buddha in both poems (C.A.F. Rhys Davids, *Brethren*, pp. 22–23 and 55–57).
14. *Therīgāthā*, vss. 57–49, 60–62, 139–144, 182–180, 189–195, 196–203, 224–235, 338–365, 366–399, 448–522.
15. *Theragāthā* vss. 350–354, 435–440, 459–465, 557–566, 705–725, 1146–1208.
16. *Saṃyutta Nikāya* I, 128–135, trans. by C.A.F. Rhys Davids, *Kindred Sayings* 1, pp. 160–170. Rhys Davids also includes a translation in her *Psalms of the Sisters* as an Appendix (pp. 180–191). Significantly, this *sutta* follows directly after the *Māra Sutta*.
17. *Theragāthā*, vss. 10, 11, 12, 35, 39, 40, 56, 68, 71, 74, 84, 92, 129, 138, 142, 154, 195, 202, 210, 227, 239, 257, 263, 282, 306, 364, 392, 457, 502ff., 576, 586, 636ff., 676ff., 704, 711ff., 990ff., 1162ff., 1214.
18. In these references to 'fools', I include those verses that refer directly to fools (*dummedha*, *manda*, or *bāla*) or to 'blind, ordinary individuals (*andhabhūta puthujjana*). *Theragāthā*, vss. 17, 37, 61, 63, 75, 84, 98, 99, 101, 106, 109, 129, 133, 146, 152, 215, 275ff., 281, 291ff., 297, 316, 341, 444, 453, 470, 518, 575, 617, 667ff., 773, 883, 1075, 1204.
19. *Therīgāthā*, vss. 240, 353, 369, 451ff., 470ff.
20. Trainor, 'In the Eye of the Beholder'.
21. In her comparative analysis of the *Therīgāthā* and *Theragāthā*, Karen Lang argues that the texts' use of vocationally oriented images implies gender distinctions in the audience towards which the verses were directed; see 'Lord Death's Snare: Gender-Related Imagery in the *Theragāthā* and the *Therīgāthā*,' p. 77. As I will discuss further in the Conclusion, my findings tend to support this contention.

Chapter II: Looking Backward

1. C.A.F. Rhys Davids, *Sisters*, p. 21.
2. For discussion and textual references, see Horner, *The Early Buddhist Theory of Man Perfected*, p. 109.
3. *Mahavāgga* I,6.32–34.
4. According to I.B. Horner, the time span between the Buddha's *nibbāna* and his institution of the *bhikkhunī-sangha* was five years; see *Women Under Primitive Buddhism*, p. 98. The story appears twice in Pali texts, in the *Aṅguttara Nikāya* (AN IV, 274–279) and in *Cullavagga X*. My summary is based on *Cullavagga X*.
5. According to I.B. Horner, this the only recorded instance of the Buddha being out-argued in Pali texts; see *Women Under Primitive Buddhism*, p. 105.
6. Many scholars assume that the story (or parts therein) must be late because of its inconsistent portrayal of women. For example, I.B. Horner attributes the Buddha's prediction of the decline of the *dhamma* to editors and redactors who introduced their own misogynist assumptions (*Women Under Primitive Buddhism*, p. xx and 105). Other scholars follow her lead. See Cornelia Dimmitt Church, 'Temptress, Housewife, Nun: Women's Role in Early Buddhism,' *Anima* 1 (1975): 52–58, p. 54, Nancy Schuster Barnes, 'Buddhism' (in Sharma, *Women in World Religions*, pp. 105–133), p. 107, Alan Sponberg, 'Attitudes Toward Women and the Feminine in Early Buddhism' (in Çabezón, *Buddhism, Sexuality, and Gender,*), p. 22, Rita Gross, *Buddhism After Patriarchy*, p. 34, and, especially Kajiyama Yuichi, 'Women in Buddhism,' *The Eastern Buddhist* 15 (1982): 53–70. Kajiyama argues that the Buddha's prediction of the decline of the *dhamma* in 500 years is a marker for the date of the text: 500 years after the death of the Buddha. But this prediction (or the similes which explain it) appears in the *Vinayas* of every school of Buddhism still extant, and must, therefore, be treated as part of the earliest strata of Buddhist literature. See Jan Nattier, *Once Upon a Future Time* (Berkeley: Asian Humanities Press, 1991), pp. 30–33 for a refutation of Kajiyama's argument and a schema of the division between schools regarding this prediction. I think, however, that Nattier is also mistaken in not attributing the prediction to the *bhikṣuṇī-vinaya* of the Mahāsāṃghika-Lokottaravādins. See Gustav Roth (ed.), *Bhikṣuṇī-Vinaya: Including Bhikṣuṇī-Prakīrṇaka and a Summary of the Bhikṣu-Prakīrṇaka of the Ārya-Mahāsāṃghika-Lokottaravādin* (Patna: K.P. Jayaswal Reasearch Institute, 1970), p. 16, section 12.

7. See Akira Hirakawa (trans.), *Monastic Discipline for the Buddhist Nuns: An English Translation of the Chinese Text of the Mahāsāṃghika-Bhikṣuṇī-Vinaya* (Patna: Kashi Prasad Jayaswal Research Institute, 1982), pp. 47–48 and Nattier, *Once Upon a Future Time*, p. 29. For a discussion, see the Introduction of Roth, *Bhikṣuṇī-Vinaya*, pp. xxx–xxxi.
8. Tessa Bartholomeusz, *Women Under the Bo Tree: Buddhist Nuns in Sri Lanka* (Cambridge: Cambridge University Press, 1994), pp. 137–138 and the dissertation on which the book is based, idem, 'Women Under the Bo Tree' (Ph.D. Dissertation, University of Virginia, 1991), pp. 50–63, Richard Gombrich and Gananath Obeyesekere, *Buddhism Transformed: Religious Change in Sri Lanka* (Princeton: Princeton University Press, 1988), p. 291, and Nancy Barnes 'Women in Buddhism,' in Arvind Sharma (ed.), *Today's Woman in World Religions* (Albany: State University of New York Press, 1994), pp.142–143.
9. Teitaro Suzuki, 'The First Buddhist Council,' *Monist* 14 (1904): 253–283, p. 265.
10. See Charles Prebish, 'A Review of Scholarship on the Buddhist Councils,' *Journal of Asian Studies* 35 (1974): 239–254 for a summary of scholarship in this area.
11. See references in note. 25 of the Introduction.
12. Cited by the first verse of the poem: *Therīgāthā* 11, 18, 25, 51, 63, 72, 87, 97, 102, 107, 122, 127, 133, 145, 151, 163, 213, 224, 252, 291, 312, 338, 400, 448.
13. By first verse of the poem: *Theragāthā* 43, 64, 72, 97, 108, 157, 219, 240, 283, 299, 340, 345, 375, 423, 429, 473, 510, 557, 620, 632, 842, 866, 892, 1091, 1209.
14. By the first verse of the poem: *Therīgāthā* 11, 18, 51, 63, 97, 102, 122, 127, 133, 151, 163, 213, 224, 271, 291, 312, 400, 448.
15. By first verse of the poem: *Theragāthā* 64, 72, 240, 299, 423, 473, 510, 557, 620, 892, 1091.
16. For translations that evoke more of an emotional response, see Rhys Davids, *Sisters*, pp. 108–110 or, especially, Susan Murcott's clear translation into colloquial English, *The First Buddhist Women: Translations and Commentary on the Therīgāthā*, pp. 87–88.
17. Cited by the first verse of the poem: *Therīgāthā* 18, 51, 97, 127, 133, 163, 204, 213, 312.
18. *Therīgāthā* 289, 300, 327.
19. By first verse: *Theragāthā* 177, 299, 512.
20. My translation, adapted from K.R. Norman. The awkward phrasing 'free am I, by being freed by means of...' is intended to

preserve the instrumental sense of *muttiyā*. Muttā's freedom is achieved by means of the three crooked things, i.e., by her meditation on them. In contrast, Sumaṅgala's freedom has an ablative sense. He is freed from them, not by means of them.

21. My translation. I translated this and the previous verse to highlight the identical phrasing in the Pali. Both Norman and Rhys Davids vary their translations according to whether they are translating the *therīs*' or the *theras*' verses. Norman translates *sumuttā* as 'well-released' for the *therīs* (11 and 23) and as 'well-rid' for the *thera* (43). Rhys Davids translates the *therīs* as 'free' (11) or 'set free' (23) but 'well-rid' for the *thera*. Apparently, even we in the modern age are not exempt from gender assumptions – 'well-rid' conveys much more personal autonomy (stereotypically associated with men) than the more passive (stereotypically feminine) 'well-released'.
22. Cited by the first verse of the poem: *Therīgāthā* 51, 63, 87, 97, 102, 107, 124, 135, 148, 154, 224, 236, 271, 291, 312, 340, 448.
23. By first verse: *Theragāthā* 287, 340, 345, 375, 423, 473, 480, 510, 557, 620, 705, 818, 866.
24. There is some indication of family resistance to the *theras*' decision to renounce. Sānu asks his mother not to cry for him (44), Ātuma mentions his wife's resistance (72), and Cūḷapanthaka is turned away by his brother (557). But, overal, the *theras* appear to encounter little difficulty.
25. *Theragāthā* vss. 63, 97, 102, 124, 236, 271, 291, 312.
26. *Therīgāthā* vss. 287, 340, 375, 426, 473, 485, 510, 620, 836, 866.
27. *Theragāthā* vss. 51, 107, 135, 148, 154.
28. In my calculations, I did not include the narrator's interjections or instructions addressed to the ascribed authors. Cited by the first verse of the poems: *Therīgāthā* 51, 54, 57, 60, 139, 182, 189, 196, 204, 224, 236, 271, 291, 312, 338, 366, 400, 448.
29. *Theragāthā* vss. 14, 25, 44, 175, 255, 335, 350, 429, 435, 459, 473, 480, 557, 8597, 705, 866, 949, 1146.
30. Even this low percentage may be artificially high. I included in my calculation every poem that contained even a very abstract, or attenuated 'conversation'. For example, Kaludayin's description of the changing season is addressed to 'lord' (527–36) and Mahāmoggallāna's poem contains several disjointed responses to various adversaries, such as his vituperative diatribe against someone he refers to as a 'bag of dung' (1150–53, ascribed by Dhammapāla to a courtesan).
31. I am indebted to Kevin Trainor for pointing out this detail. 'In the Eye of the Beholder,' p. 64.

32. *Therīgāthā* vss. 8, 43, 67, 119, 125, 127, 170, 178, 204, 331, 363, 400, 518.
33. *Theragāthā* vss. 4, 14, 56, 75, 148, 179, 209, 249, 264, 330, 335, 402, 429, 648, 660, 681, 949, 993, 1018, 1209.
34. Rhys Davids follows the commentary in ascribing the benediction to Sundarī's mother, arguing that the tone of the verse reflects a lay perspective (C.A.F. Rhys Davids, *Sisters*, n. 3, p. 139). I think it is unnecessary to impose a chronological break between a coherent dialogue that is clearly addressed by Sundarī to the 'beauty of the order of *therīs*'.
35. *Theragāthā* vss. 4, 75, 147, 249, 264, 387, 505, 610, 981–1017, 1018–19.
36. The following verses use the terms *eka, paviveka, vivitta* ('solitude') to refer to the ascribed author. I have included only one verse per poem, though several repeat the vocabulary and imagery of solitude. *Theragāthā* vss. 6, 23, 27, 49, 54, 62, 110, 142, 149, 189, 233, 239, 245, 537, 577, 592, 597, 626, 669, 726, 848, 896, 920, 981, 1036, 1091, 1168. In my calculation, I also include vss. 76 ('one should remain when others are not remaining'), 494 ('one should avoid people'), and 1051 (' One should not approve of a crowd') though they do not use the same vocabulary.
37. *Therīgāthā* vss. 57, 230, 372–3.

Chapter III: Looking Inward

1. C.A.F. Rhys Davids, *Sisters*, p.56.
2. Diana Paul, *Women in Buddhism*, p. 5.
3. Nancy Falk, 'An Image of Woman in Old Buddhist Literature' (in Plaskow and Arnold, *Women and Religion*), p. 110.
4. I.B. Horner (trans.), *The Book of Discipline*, Vol. V (London: Luzac and Co. Ltd., 1952), p. 356.
5. See John Ross Carter, *Dhamma: Western Academic and Sinhalese Buddhist Interpretations, A Study of a Religious Concept* (Tokyo: The Hokuseido Press, 1978).
6. Horner, *The Book of Discipline*, Vol. I, pp. 36–37.
7. *Vinaya* III, iv, 210–212.
8. Horner, *The Book of Discipline*, Vol. I, pp. 36–37.
9. F.L. Woodward (trans.), *The Book of Gradual Sayings*, Vol. III (London: Luzac and Co. Ltd., 1932), pp. 55–57.
10. *Ibid.*, Vol. in, III, p. 56. See Karen Lang's article, 'Lord Death's Snare: Gender-related Imagery in the *Thera*- and *Therīgāthā*,' for an analysis of this snare imagery in the *Therīgāthā* and *Theragāthā*.

11. Some scholars argue that this type of presentation should be considered an aberation rather than the norm. They base this conclusion on a hypothetical chronology of passages in the Pali texts. According to this chronology, the passages that present a more egalitarian image of the early *sangha* must logically predate more misogynist passages as it is hard to imagine how egalitarianism could have evolved in such a setting. It is much easier to envision the decline of an initially equal situation. See, for example, Kevin Trainor, 'In the Eye of the Beholder,' Alan Sponberg, 'Attitudes towards the Feminine in Early Buddhism,' and Rita Gross, *Buddhism After Patriarchy.*
12. Thanks to Kevin Trainor for allowing me to read a draft of his paper, 'In the Eye of the Beholder' which steered me to the 'Discourse on the Setting Up of Mindfulness' in the *Dīgha Nikāya*, Vol. II, pp. 327–346.
13. C.A.F. Rhys Davids, *Sisters*, pp. 22–23 and 55.
14. C.A.F. Rhys Davids, *Brethren*, p. 383; C.A.F. Rhys Davids, *Sisters*, p. 52.
15. C.A. F. Rhys Davids, *Brethren*, p. 179.
16. *Theragāthā* vss. 281, 316, 394, 454, 738, 1153. See also the analysis of fools attracted to the painted puppet below.
17. See Karen Lang's article, 'Lord Death's Snare: Gender-Related Imagery in the *Theragāthā* and the *Therīgāthā*,' for a detailed discussion of the use of this imagery in the texts and commentary.
18. *Ibid.*, p. 78.
19. *Ibid.*, p. 77.
20. C.A.F. Rhys Davids, *Brethren*, p. 353.
21. *Theragāthā* vss. 30, 108, 118, 283, 405, 411, 450, 518, 1039, 1093.
22. *Therīgāthā* vss. 16, 27, 29, 67, 95, 102, 110, 252, 493.
23. Siegfried Lienhard, 'Sur la Structure Poetique des Thera-Therīgāthā,' pp. 379–80.
24. Thanks to Graeme MacQueen for suggesting this distinction between 'romantic' and 'medical' perceptions of the body.
25. See for example, the *Mahāparinibbāna sutta* in the *Dīgha Nikāya* II, 64, 109, or the commentary, C.A.F. Rhys Davids, *Sisters*, p. 120.

Chapter IV: Looking Outward

1. A slightly adapted translation by C.A.F. Rhys Davids, *Sisters*, p. 252.

2. For example, see Sukumar Dutt, *Buddhist Monks and Monasteries of India* (London; George Allen and Unwin Ltd, 1962), pp. 54–57.
3. *Khaggavisāṇasutta*, vs. 39. Trans. by Ria Kloppenborg, *The Paccekabuddha: A Buddhist Ascetic* (Leiden: E.J. Brill, 1974), p. 91.
4. For a thorough discussion of similar uses of this imagery, see Steven Collins, *Selfless Persons: Imagery and Thought in Theravāda Buddhism*, pp. 167–171.
5. See E.B. Cowell (trans.), *The Buddha-carita of Aśvaghoṣa*, Vol. XLIX of *Sacred Books of the East*, ed. by F. Max Müller (Oxford: Clarendon Press, 1894; reprint; New York: Dover Publications, Inc., 1969).
6. Horner, *Women Under Primitive Buddhism*, p. 154.
7. *Cullavagga* X, 23, as cited in *Women Under Primitive Buddhism*, p. 155. Horner notes that this may be a different Uppalavaṇṇā than appears in the *Therīgāthā*.
8. *Ibid*., p. 156, citing the *Vinaya* IV, p. 264.
9. C.A.F. Rhys Davids, 'The Love of Nature in Buddhist Poems,' pp. 432–433. For another study of nature imagery in the *Therīgāthā* and *Theragāthā*, see B.G. Gokhale, 'The Image-World of the *Thera-Therī-gāthās*.'
10. Oldenberg, *Literatur des alten Indien*, p. 101, as cited by Winternitz, *A History of Indian Literature*, Vol. II (New York: Russell and Russell, 1933), n. 3, pp. 102–103.
11. *Women Under Primitive Buddhism*, p. 209.
12. I recognize that some of these 'settings' could be interpreted as metaphors for liberation, but, even if this is the case, the metaphoric use of environmental imagery as setting still presents a topographical emphasis that differs between the texts. Furthermore, even if we were to accept settings as metaphors, my findings would not be that different. Thanks to Ellen Badone for pointing out the possibility of this interpretation.
13. Cited by the first verse of their poems, the liberated *theras* for whom forest or trees are a setting are *Theragāthā* 6, 55, 217, 435, 466, 537, 557, 597, 620, 842, 866, 892, 920, 1051, 1146.
14. Cited by the first verse of their poems: *Therīgāthā* 23, 51, 72, 77, 145, 224, 338, 366.
15. *Theragāthā* 1, 51, 52, 53, 54, 55, 56, 58, 59, 60, 127, 325, and 487.
16. C.A.F. Rhys Davids, *Brethren*, p. 391.
17. This use of fire symbolism has an obvious relationship with the Buddha's famous 'fire sermon', *Mahāvagga* I, 21.

Chapter V: Struggle for Liberation in the *Therīgāthā*

1. C.A.F. Rhys Davids, *Sisters*, pp. 45–46.
2. For a study of this juxtaposition of secular and devotional sections of the poems, see Lienhard, 'Sur la Structure Poetique des Thera-Therīgāthā.'
3. M. Winternitz, *A History of Indian Literature*, Vol. II, p. 102.
4. Kristin Wardetsky, 'The Structure and Interpretation of Fairy Tales Composed by Children,' p. 168.
5. *Ibid.*, p. 164.
6. *Ibid.*, p. 169.
7. *Ibid.*
8. Caroline Walker Bynum, 'Women's Stories, Women's Symbols: A Critique of Victor Turner's Theory of Liminality.' (in Moore and Reynolds, *Anthropology and the Study of Religion*), pp. 105–125.
9. Caroline Walker Bynum, '"And Woman His Humanity": Female Imagery in the Religious Writing of the Later Middle Ages' (in Bynum, *Gender and Religion: On the Complexity of Symbols*), pp. 257–288.
10. John Stratton Hawley, 'Images of Gender in the Poetry of Krishna' (in Bynum, *Gender and Religion: On the Complexity of Symbols*), pp. 231–256.
11. *Ibid.*, pp. 237–238.
12. *Ibid.*, p. 240.
13. *Ibid.*, p. 243.

BIBLIOGRAPHY

Reference Works

Apte, V.S. *The Practical Sanskrit-English Dictionary*. Vols. I–III. Poona: Prasad Prakashan, 1957.

Edgerton, Franklin. *Buddhist Hybrid Sanskrit Grammar and Dictionary*. Vols. I and II. New Haven: Yale University Press, 1953; (reprint) Delhi: Motilal Banarsidass, 1970.

Johansson, Rune. *Pali Buddhist Texts: Explained to the Beginner*. 2nd ed. Oxford: Curzon Press, 1977.

Joshi, C.V. *A Manual of Pali*. Poona: Oriental Book Agency, 1964.

Monier-Williams, Sir Monier. *A Sanskrit-English Dictionary*. Revised edition. Delhi: Motilal Banarsidass, 1963.

Rhys Davids, T.W. and William Stede (eds.). *The Pali Text Society's Pali-English Dictionary*. London: The Pali Text Society, 1921–25.

Upasak, Chandrika Singh. *Dictionary of Early Buddhist Monastic Terms Based on Pali Literature*. Varanasi: Bharati Prakashan, 1975.

Witney, William. *Sanskrit Grammar*, 2nd ed. London: Oxford University Press, 1889; (reprint) 1967.

——. *The Roots, Verb-forms, and Primary Derivatives of the Sanskrit Language*. London: Trubner and Co., 1885; (reprint) The American Oriental Society, 1988.

Texts and Translations

Hardy, E. (ed.). *Aṅguttara Nikāya*. London: Luzac and Co., 1958.

Horner, I.B. (trans.). *The Book of the Discipline*, Parts I–V. London: Luzac and Co. Ltd., 1949–1963.

Norman, K.R. (trans.). *Elders' Verses*, Vols. I–II. London: Luzac and Co. Ltd., 1969–1971.

Oldenberg, Hermann (ed.). *The Vinaya Piṭakaṃ*, Vols. I–V. London: Luzac and Co. Ltd., 1879–1883.

Oldenberg, Hermann and Richard Pischel (eds.). *Thera-Therī-Gāthā;* 2nd edition with appendices by K.R. Norman and L. Alsdorf, London: Luzac and Co., 1966.

Rhys Davids, C.A.F. (trans.). *Psalms of the Early Buddhists*. London: Luzac and Co., 1909–1913; (reprint) 1964.

Ridding, C.M. and La Vallée Poussin, Louis de (eds.). 'A Fragment of the Sanskrit Vinaya: *Bhikṣuṇīkarma-vacana*.' *Bulletin of the School of Oriental and African Studies* 113 (1919): 123–143.

Roth, Gustav (ed.). *Bhikṣuṇī-Vinaya: Including Bhikṣuṇī-Prakīrṇaka and a Summary of the Bhikṣu-Prakīrṇaka of the Ārya-Mahāsāṃghika-Lokottaravādin*. Patna: K.P. Jayaswal Reasearch Institute, 1970.

Scholarship on the *Therī-Therīgāthā*

Gokhale, Balakrishna Govind. 'The Image-World of the *Thera-Therī-Gāthās*.' In *Malalasekara Commemoration Volume*, ed. by D.H. De A. Wijesekera. Colombo: Kularatne and Co. Ltd., 1976, pp. 96–110.

Lang, Karen. 'Images of Women in Early Buddhism and Christian Gnosticism.' *Buddhist and Christian Studies* 2 (1982): 95–105.

——. 'Lord Death's Snare: Gender-Related Imagery in the *Theragāthā* and the *Therīgāthā*.' *Journal of Feminist Studies in Religion* 2 (1986): 63–79.

Lienhard, Siegfried. 'Sur la Structure Poetique des *Thera-Therīgāthā*. '*Journal Asiatique* 263 (1975): 375–396.

Murcott, Susan. *The First Buddhist Women: Translations and Commentary on the Therīgāthā*. Berkeley: Parallax Press, 1991.

Rhys Davids, C.A.F. 'The Love of Nature in Buddhist Poems.'*The Quest: A Quarterly Review* 1 (April, 1910): 416–434.

Sharma, Arvind. 'How and Why Did the Women in Ancient India Become Buddhist Nuns?' *Sociological Analysis* 38 (1977): 239–251.

Stede, William. 'The Pādas of the *Thera*- and *Therī-gāthā*.'*Journal of the Pali Text Society* 1924–27, pp. 31–226.

Trainor, Kevin. 'In the Eye of the Beholder: Nonattachment and the Body in Subhā's Verse (*Therīgāthā* 71).' *Journal of the American Academy of Religion* 61 (1993): 57–79.

Scholarship on Women in Buddhism

Amarasingham Lorna Rhodes. 'The Misery of the Embodied: Representations of Women in Sinhalese Myth.' In *Women in*

Ritual and Symbolic Roles, ed. by Judith Hoch-Smith and Anita Spring. New York: Plenum Press, 1978, pp. 101–126.

Balbir, Nalini. 'Women in Jainism.' In *Religion and Women*, ed. by Arvin Sharma. Albany: State University of New York Press, 1994, pp. 121–138.

Barnes, Nancy Schuster. 'Buddhism.' In *Women in World Religions*, ed. by Arvind Sharma. Albany: State University of New York Press, 1987, pp. 105–133.

——. 'Women in Buddhism.' In *Today's Woman in World Religions*, ed. by Arvind Sharma. Albany: State University of New York Press, 1994, pp. 137–169.

Bartholomeusz, Tessa. 'The Female Mendicant in Buddhist Sri Lanka.' In *Buddhism, Sexuality, and Gender*, ed. by José Ignacio Cabezón. Albany: State University of New York Press, 1992, pp. 37–61.

——. 'Women Under the Bo Tree.' Ph.D. Dissertation, University of Virginia, 1991.

——. *Women Under The Bo Tree: Buddhist Nuns in Sri Lanka*. Cambridge: Cambridge University Press, 1994.

Bloss, Lowell. 'The Female Renunciants of Sri Lanka: The *Dasasilmattawa*.' *Journal of the International Association of Buddhist Studies* 10 (1987): 7–31.

Bode, Mabel. 'Women Leaders of the Buddhist Reformation.' *Journal of the Royal Asiatic Society* 25 (1893): 517–566; 763–798.

Cabezón, José Ignacio (ed.). *Buddhism, Sexuality, and Gender*. Albany: State University of New York Press, 1992.

Church, Cornelia Dimmitt. 'Temptress, Housewife, Nun: Women's Role in Early Buddhism.' *Anima* 1 (1975): 52–58.

Falk, Nancy. 'The Case of the Vanishing Nuns: The Fruits of Ambivalence in Ancient Indian Buddhism.' In *Unspoken Worlds: Women's Religious Lives in Non- Western Cultures*, ed. by N. Falk and Rita Gross. San Fransisco: Harper and Row, 1980, pp. 207–224.

——. 'To Gaze on the Sacred Traces.' *History of Religions* 16 (1977): 281–293.

——. 'An Image of Woman in Old Buddhist Literature: The Daughters of *Māra*.' In *Women and Religion*, ed. by Judith Plaskow and Joan Arnold. Missoula: Scholars Press, 1974, pp. 105–112.

Gross, Rita. 'The Householder and the World-Renunciant: Two Modes of Sexual Expression in Buddhism.' *Journal of Ecumenical Studies* 22 (1985): 81–96.

——. *Buddhism After Patriarchy: A Feminist History, Analysis, and Reconstruction of Buddhism*. Albany: State University of New York Press, 1993.

Harrison, Paul. 'Who Gets to Ride in the Great Vehicle? Self-Image and Identity Among the Followers of the Early Mahāyāna.' *Journal of the International Association of Buddhist Studies* 10 (1987): 67–89.

Hiroko Kawanami. 'The Religious Standing of Burmese Buddhist Nuns (*thila-shin*): The Ten Precepts and Religious Respect Words.' *Journal of the International Association of Buddhist Studies* 13 (1987): 17–39.

Horner, I.B. *Women Under Primitive Buddhism*. London, 1930; (reprint) Delhi: Motilal Banarsidass, 1975.

——. *Women in Early Buddhist Literature*. Kandy: Buddhist Publication Society, 1961.

Jaini, Padmanabh. *Gender and Salvation: Jaina Debates on the Spiritual Liberation of Women*. Berkeley: University of California Press, 1991.

——. *Padipadanajātaka*: Gautama's Last Female Incarnation.' In *Amala Prajñā: Aspects of Buddhist Studies*, ed. by N.H. Samanti and H.S. Prasad. Delhi: Indian Books Centre, 1989, pp. 33–39.

De Jong, J.W. 'Notes on the *Bhikṣuṇī-Vinaya* of the Mahāsāṃghikas.' In *Buddhist Studies in Honour of I.B. Horner*, ed. by L. Cousins, et al. Dordrecht-Holland: D. Reidel Publishing Co, 1974, pp. 63–70.

Gombrich, Richard. 'Feminine Elements in Sinhalese Buddhism.' *Wiener Zeitschrift für die Kunde Südasiens und Archiv fur Indische Philosophie* 14–16 (1970–72): 67–93.

Kabilsingh, Chatsumarn. *A Comparative Study of Bhikkhunī Pāṭimokkha*. Varanasi: Chaukhambha Orientalia, 1984.

Kajiyama Yuichi, 'Women in Buddhism.' *Eastern Buddhist* 15 (1982): 53–70.

Keyes, Charles. 'Mother or Mistress But Never a Monk: Buddhist Notions of Female Gender in Rural Thailand.' *American Ethnologist* 11 (1984): 223–241.

Ku, Cheng-Mei. 'Mahāyānic View of Women: A Doctrinal Study.' Ph.D. Dissertation, University of Wisconsin, 1984.

Nissan, Elizabeth. 'Recovering Practice: Buddhist Nuns in Sri Lanka.' *South Asia Research* 4 (1984): 32–49.

Paul, Diana. 'Buddhist Attitudes Toward Women's Bodies.' *Buddhist-Christian Studies* 1 (1988): 63–71.

——. *Women in Buddhism: Images of the Feminine in the Mahāyāna Tradition*. Berkeley: University of California Press, 1979.

Richman, Paula. 'Gender and Persuasion.' In *Buddhism, Sexuality, and Gender*, ed. by José Ignacio Cabezón. New York: State University of New York Press, 1992, pp. 111–136.

——. 'The Portrayal of a Female Renouncer in a Tamil Buddhist Text.' In *Gender and Religion: On the Complexity of Symbols*, ed. by C. Walker Bynum, et al. Boston: Beacon Press, 1986, pp. 143–165.

——. *Women, Branch Stories, and Religious Rhetoric in a Tamil Buddhist Text.* Foreign and Comparative Studies, South Asia Series, Syracuse, New York: Maxwell School, Syracuse University, 1988.

Schopen, Gregory. 'On Monks, Nuns and "Vulgar" Practices: The Introduction of the Image Cult into Indian Buddhism.' *Artibus Asiae* 49 (1989): 153–168.

Sharma, Arvind. 'Can There Be a Female Buddha in Theravāda Buddhism?' In *Women, Literature, Criticism*, ed. by Harry Garvin. London: Associated University Presses, 1978, pp. 105–133.

Sponberg, Alan. 'Attitudes toward Women and the Feminine in Early Buddhism.' In *Buddhism, Sexuality, and Gender*, ed. by José Cabezón. Albany: State University of New York Press, 1992, pp. 3–36.

Stevens, John. *Lust for Enlightenment: Buddhism and Sex*. Boston: Shambhalla, 1990.

Talim, Meena. *Women in Early Buddhist Literature*. Bombay: University of Bombay, 1972.

Tsomo, Karma Lekshe (ed.). *Sakyadhita: Daughters of the Buddha*. Ithaca, N.Y.: Snow Lion Publications, 1988.

Willis, Janice D. 'Nuns and Benefactresses: The Role of Women in the Development of Buddhism.' In *Women, Religion, and Social Change*, ed. by Y. Haddad and E. Findly. Albanay: State University of New York Press, 1985, pp. 59–85.

Wilson, Frances. 'The Nun.' Chapter III of *Women in Buddhism*, by Diana Paul. Berkeley: University of California Press 1979, pp. 77–105.

Scholarship on Buddhism

Bechert, Heinz. 'Methodological Considerations Concerning the Language of the Earliest Buddhist Tradition.' *Buddhist Studies Review* 6 (1991): 3–19.

Boyd, James W. 'The Theravāda View of *Saṃsāra*.' In *Buddhist Studies in Honour of Walpola Rahula*, ed. by S. Balasooriya, et al. London: Gordon Fraser, 1980, pp. 29–43.

Burford, Grace. 'The Ideal Goal According to the *Aṭṭhaka-vagga* and its Major Pali Commentaries.' Ph.D. Dissertation, Northwestern University, 1983.

Carrithers, Michael. *The Forest Monks of Sri Lanka*. Delhi: Oxford University Press, 1983.

——. 'Hell-Fire and Urinal Stones: An Essay on Buddhist Purity and Authority.' In *Contributions to South Asian Studies* II. ed. by Gopal Krishna. Delhi: Oxford University Press, 1982, pp. 25–52.

Carter, John Ross. *Dhamma: Western Academic and Sinhalese Buddhist Interpretations, A Study of a Religious Concept*. Tokyo: The Hokuseido Press, 1978.

——. 'Traditional Definitions of the term *Dhamma*.' *Philosophy East and West* 26 (1976): 329–337.

Chakravarti, Uma. *The Social Dimensions of Early Buddhism*. Delhi:Oxford University Press, 1987.

——. 'The Social Philosophy of Buddhism and the Problem of Inequality.' *Social Compass* 32 (1986): 199–221.

Clasquin, Michel. 'Contemporary Theravada and Zen Buddhist Attitudes to Human Sexuality: An Exercise in Comparative Ethics.' *Religion* 22 (1992): 63–63.

Collins, Steven. 'Monasticism, Utopias and Comparative Social Theory.' *Religion* 18 (1988): 101–135.

——. '*Nirvāṇa*, Time, and Narrative.' *History of Religions* 31 (1992): 215–246.

——. 'Notes on Some Oral Aspects of Pali Literature.' *Indo-Iranian Journal* 35 (1992): 121–135.

——. 'On the Very Idea of the Pali Canon.' *Journal of the Pali Text Society* 15 (1990): 89–126.

——. *Selfless Persons: Imagery and Thought in Theravāda Buddhism*. Cambridge: Cambridge University Press, 1982.

Dutt, Nalinaksha. *Buddhist Sects in India*. Calcutta: Calcutta Oriental Press (Pvt.) Ltd., 1970.

——. *Early Monastic Buddhism*. Calcutta: Calcutta Oriental Book Agency, 1941.

Dutt, Sukumar. *Buddhist Monks and Monasteries of India: Their History and Their Contribution to Indian Culture*. London: George Allen and Unwin Ltd., 1962.

Findly, Ellison Banks. 'Ānanda's Hindrance: Faith (*Saddhā*) in Early Buddhism.' *Journal of Indian Philosophy* 20 (1992): 253–273.

Frauwallner, Erich. *The Earliest Vinaya and the Beginnings of Buddhist Literature*. Volume VIII of Serie Orientale Roma. Rome: Instituto per il Medio ed Estremo Oriente, 1956.

Freedman, Michael. 'The Characterization of Ānanda in the Pali Canon of the Theravāda: A Hagiographic Study.' Ph.D. Dissertation, McMaster University, 1977.

Geiger, Wilhelm. *Pali Literature and Language*. Trans. by Batakrishna Ghosh. New Delhi: Oriental Books Reprint Corporation, 1943.

Gombrich, Richard. 'The Buddha's Book of Genesis?' *Indo-Iranian Journal* 35 (1992): 159–178.

——. 'Making Mountains Without Molehills: The Case of the Missing *Stūpa*.' *Journal of the Pali Text Society* 15 (1990): 141–143.

——. 'Recovering the Buddha's Message.' In *The Buddhist Forum – Vol I: Seminar Papers 1987–88*, ed. by Tadeusz Skorupski. New Delhi: Heritage Publishers, School of Oriental and African Studies, 1990.

——. *Theravāda Buddhism: A Social History from Ancient Benares to Modern Colombo*. London: Routledge, 1988.

Gombrich, Richard and Gananath Obeyesekere. *Buddhism Transformed: Religious Change in Sri Lanka*. Princeton: Princeton University Press, 1988.

Hallisey, Charles. 'Appropos the Pali Vinaya as a Historical Document: A Reply to Gregory Schopen.' *Journal of the Pali Text Society* 15 (1990): 197–208.

Hinüber, Oskar von. '*Khandhakavatta*: Loss of Text in the Pali *Vinayapiṭaka*?' *Journal of the Pali Text Society* 15 (1990): 127–138.

Holt, John. *Discipline: The Canonical Buddhism of the Vinayapiṭaka*. Delhi: Motilal Banarsidass, 1983.

Horner, I.B. *The Early Buddhist Theory of Man Perfected: A Study of the Arahan Concept and of the Implications of the Aim to Perfection in Religious Life*, 1936; (reprint) Amsterdam: Phijo Press, 1975.

Johansson, Rune. *The Psychology of Nirvāṇa*. London: George Allen and Unwin, Ltd., 1969.

Kloppenborg, Ria. *The Paccekabuddha: A Buddhist Ascetic*. Leiden: E.J. Brill, 1974.

La Vallée Poussin, Louis de. 'The Buddhist Councils.' *Indian Antiquary* 38 (1908): 1–18; 81–106.

——. 'Councils (Buddhist).' In the *Encyclopaedia of Religion and Ethics*, Volume IV: pp. 179–185.

Lamotte, Étienne. 'The Assessment of Textual Interpretation in Buddhism.' Trans. by Sara Webb-Boin. *Buddhist Studies Review* 1 (1983): 4–15.

——. *History of Indian Buddhism: From the Origins to the Śaka Era*. Trans. by Sara Webb-Boin from the French, Louvain, 1958, Louvain-La-Neuve: Institut Orientaliste, 1988.

——. 'Passions and Impregnations of the Passions in Buddhism.' In *Buddhist Studies in Honour of I.B. Horner*, ed. by L. Cousins, et al. Dordrecht-Holland: C. Reidel Publishing Co., 1974, pp. 91–104.

Law, Bimila Churn. *A History of Pali Literature* Vol. II. London: Kegan Paul, Trench, Trubner and Co. Ltd., 1933.

Macy, Joanna Rogers. 'Dependent Co-arising: The Distinctiveness of Buddhist Ethics.' *Journal of Religious Ethics* 7 (1979): 38–52.

Majumdar, Ramesh Chandra. 'The First Council.' In *Buddhistic Studies*, ed. by B.C. Law. Calcutta: Thacker, Spink, 1931, pp. 26–72.

Malalasekera, G.P. *The Pali Literature of Ceylon*. Colombo: M.D. Gunasena, 1928.

Manné, Joy. 'Categories of *Sutta* in the Pali *Nikāyas* and their Implications for our Appreciation of the Buddhist Teaching and Literature.' *Journal of the Pali Text Society* 15 (1990): 29–87.

Masefield, Peter. *Divine Revelation in Pali Buddhism*. London: George Allen and Unwin, 1986.

McDermott, James P. 'Scripture as the Word of the Buddha.' *Numen* 31 (1984): 22–39.

Nattier, Jan. *Once Upon a Future Time: Studies in a Buddhist Prophecy of Decline*. Berkeley: Asian Humanities Press, 1991.

Nattier, Jan and Charles Prebish. 'Mahāsāṃghika Origins: The Beginnings of Buddhist Sectarianism.' *History of Religions* 16 (1977): 237–272.

Norman, K.R. *Pali Literature*. Wiesbaden: Otto Harrassowitz, 1983.

——. 'Pali Philology and the Study of Buddhism.' In *The Buddhist Forum – Vol. I: Seminar Papers 1987–88*, ed. by Tadeusz Skorupski. New Delhi: Heritage Publishers, School of Oriental and African Studies, 1990, pp. 31–39.

Prebish, Charles. *Buddhist Monastic Discipline: The Sanskrit Prātimokṣa Sūtras of the Mahāsāṃghikas and Mūlasarvāstivādins*. University Park: Pennsylvania State University Press, 1975.

——. 'Recent Progress in Vinaya Studies.' In *Studies in Pali Buddhism*, ed. by A. K. Narain. Delhi: B.R. Publishing Co., 1979, pp. 297–306.

——. 'A Review of Scholarship on the Buddhist Councils.' *Journal of Asian Studies* 35 (1974): 239–254.

——. *A Survey of Vinaya Literature*. Vol. I of the Dharma Lamp Series. Taiwan: Jin Luen Publishing House, 1994.

Roth, Gustav. '*Bhikṣuṇīvinaya* and *Bhikṣu-Prakīrṇaka* and Notes on the Language.' *Journal of the Bihar Research Society* 52 (1966): 29–51.

——. 'Notes on the Introduction of the *Bhikṣu-Prātimokṣa-Sūtra* of the Ārya-Mahāsāṃghika-Lokottaravādin.' In *Studies in Pali and Buddhism*, ed. by A.K. Narain. Delhi: B.R. Publishing Co., 1979, pp. 317–326.

Schopen, Gregory. 'Archeology and Protestant Presuppositions in the Study of Indian Buddhism.' *History of Religions* 31 (1991): 1–23.
——. 'The *Stūpa* Cult and the Extant Pali *Vinaya*.' *Journal of the Pali Text Society* 13 (1990): 83–100.
——. 'Two Problems in the History of Indian Buddhism: The Layman/ Monk Distinction and the Doctrines of the Transference of Merit.' *Studien zur Indologie und Iranistik* 10 (1985): 9–47.
Silber, Ilana R. '"Opting Out" in Theravada Buddhism and Medieval Christianity: A Comaparative Study of Monasticism as Alternative Structure.' *Religion* 15 (1985): 251–277.
Suzuki, Teitaro. 'The First Buddhist Council.' *Monist* 14 (1904): 253–283.
Walters, Jonathan. 'The Buddha's Bad Karma: A Problem in the History of Theravāda Buddhism.' *Numen* 37 (1990): 70–95.
Warder, A.K. *Indian Buddhism*, 2nd ed. Delhi: Motilal Banarsidass, 1980.
Welbon, Guy. *The Buddhist Nirvāṇa and its Western Interpreters*. Chicago: University of Chicago Press, 1968.
Wijayaratna, Mohan. *Buddhist Monastic Life: According to the Texts of the Theravāda Tradition*. Trans. by C. Grangier and S. Collins, Cambridge: Cambridge University Press, 1990.
Williams, Raymond. 'Historical Criticism of a Buddhist Scripture: The *Mahaparinibbāna Sutta*.' *Journal of the American Academy of Religion* 38 (1970): 156–167.
Winternitz, M. *A History of Indian Literature*, Vol. II. Trans. by S. Ketkar and H. Kohn from the German. Delhi: 1933; (reprint) New York: Russell and Russell, 1971.

Theoretical Works

Basso, Ellen. 'Introduction: Discourse as an Integrating Concept in Anthropology and Folklore Research.' *Journal of Folklore Research* 27 (1990): 3–10.
Bauman, Richard. *Story, Performance and Event: Contextual Studies of Oral Narrative*. Cambridge: Cambridge University Press, 1986.
Bynum, Caroline Walker. '"And Women His Humanity": Female Imagery in the Religious Writing of the Later Middle Ages.' In *Gender and Religion: On the Complexity of Symbols*, ed. by C. Walker Bynum, Steve Harrell and Paula Richman. Boston: Beacon Press, 1986, pp. 257–288.
——. 'The Complexity of Symbols.' Introduction to *Gender and Religion: On the Complexity of Symbols*, ed. by C. Walker Bynum, Steve Harrell and Paula Richman. Boston: Beacon Press, 1986, pp. 1–20.

——. *Holy Feast and Holy Fast: The Religious Significance of Food to Medieval Women*. Berkeley: University of California Press, 1987.

——. 'Women's Stories, Women's Symbols.' In *Anthropology and the Study of Religion*, ed. by R. Moore and F. Reynolds. Chicago: Centre for the Scientific Study of Religion, 1984, pp. 105–125.

Dundes, Alan. *Interpreting Folklore*, Bloomington: Indiana University Press, 1987.

——. (ed.). *Sacred Narrative*, Berkeley: University of California Press, 1984.

Finnegan, Ruth. 'What is Oral Literature Anyway?' In *Oral Literature and the Formula*, ed. by B. Stolz and R. Shannon, Ann Arbor: University of Michigan, 1976, pp. 127–166.

Foley, John Miles. 'Word-Power, Performance, and Tradition.' *Journal of American Folklore* 105 (1992): 275–301.

Geertz, Clifford. 'Religion as a Cultural System.' Chapter IV of *The Interpretation of Cultures*, New York: Basic Books, 1973, pp. 87–125.

Hawley, John Stratton. 'Images of Gender in the Poetry of Krishna.' In *Gender and Religion: On the Complexity of Symbols*, ed. by C. Walker Bynum, et al. Boston: Beacon Press, 1986, pp. 231–256.

Jordan, R. and S. Kalcik (eds.). *Women's Folklore, Women's Culture*. Philadelphia: University of Pennsylvania Press, 1985.

Kirshenblatt-Gimblett, Barbara. 'A Parable in Context.' In *Folklore: Performance and Communication*, ed. by Dan Ben-Amos and Kenneth Goldstein The Hague: Mouton, 1975, pp. 105–130.

Lakoff, George and Mark Johnson. *Metaphors We Live By*. Chicago: University of Chicago Press, 1980.

Lawless, Elaine. '"I was afraid someone like you … an outsider … would misunderstand": Negotiating Interpretive Differences Between Ethnographers and Subjects.' *Journal of American Folklore* 105 (1992): 302–314.

——. 'Rescripting Their Lives and Narratives: Spiritual Life Stories of Pentacostal Women Preachers.' *Journal of Feminist Studies in Religion* 7 (1991): 53–72.

Lord, Albert. *The Singer of Tales*. Cambridge: Harvard University Press, 1960.

Maraldo, John C. 'Hermeneutics and Historicity in the Study of Buddhism.' *Eastern Buddhist*, N.S. 19 (1986): 17–43.

Narayan, Kirin. *Storytellers, Saints, and Scoundrels*. Philadelphia: University of Pennsylvania Press, 1989.

Roseberg, Bruce, 'Oral Sermons and Oral Narrative.' In *Folklore: Performance and Communication*, ed. by Dan Ben-Amos and Kenneth Goldstein. The Hague: Mouton, 1975.

Stahl, Sandra. 'Literary Folkloristic Methodology for the Study of Meaning in Personal Narrative.' *Journal of Folklore Research* 22 (1985): 45–69.

——. 'The Oral Personal Narrative in its Generic Context.' *Fabula* 18 (1977) : 18–39.

——. 'Personal Experience Stories.' In *Handbook of American Folklore*, ed. by R. Dorson. Bloomington: Indiana University Press, 1983, pp. 268–276.

Wadley, Susan. 'Texts in Contexts: Oral Traditions and the Study of Religion in Karimpur.' *American Studies in the Anthropology of India*, ed. by S. Vatuk. New Delhi: Manohar, 1978, pp. 309–341.

Wardetsky, Kristin. 'The Structure and Interpretation of Fairy Tales Composed by Children.' *Journal of American Folklore* 103 (1990): 157–176.

Zelliot, Eleanor 'Buddhist Women of the Contemporary Maharashtrian Conversion Movement.' In *Buddhism, Sexuality, and Gender*, ed. by José Cabezón. New York: State University of New York Pess, 1992, pp. 91–107.

GLOSSARY

Arahant. One who has attained liberation, the religious goal of Buddhism.

Āsavas. Intoxicating influences or destructive inclinations. The term usually has a psychological connotation, implying all ideas, sensations, or tendencies that obstruct one's concentration on liberation.

Ascribed Author. The person(s) to whom a particular poem from the *Therīgāthā* or *Theragāthā* is attributed. I use this phrase or '*therī*' or '*thera*' to distinguish between the designated author and the actual authors or redactors of the texts.

Bhikkhu. An ordained male Buddhist renunciant.

Bhikkhunī. An ordained female Buddhist renunciant.

Dhamma. The teachings of the Buddha, the Truth those teachings convey, or the path to attain that Truth. *Dhamma* is one of the central religious concepts in Buddhism.

Dukkha. Literally 'pain or suffering', the term implies the dissatisfaction that characterizes the human condition. In the Buddha's teachings, even pleasure is *dukkha* because it is bound to be impermanent and it encourages us to desire more pleasure.

Gāthā. Verse, or poem. Buddhist *gāthā* follows clear conventions with regard to the number and type of syllables per verse and metric or rhythmic styles of composition.

Karma (Pali, *kamma*). Literally 'action', but it includes and implies the moral law of cause and effect. Every thought, word, or deed has consequences that will rebound upon us, either in this lifetime or in the next.

Māra. The Buddhist temptor. A being with super powers, Māra delights in turning people away from the path to liberation (the *dhamma*). The realm of *saṃsāra* (see below) is said to be Māra's realm, when it instills temptation, fear, and aversion.

Pāda. A fourth of a verse, distinguished by meter and syllable count.

Paramatthadīpanī. Dhammapāla's sixth century commentary on the *Therīgāthā* and the *Theragāthā*.

Saṃsāra. The relentless cylce of birth, death, rebirth and redeath from which Buddhist renunciants seek to extricate themselves. *Saṃsāra* characterizes the human condition, and is virtually synonymous with *dukkha*.

Sangha. The Buddhist community of renunciants.

Thera. An ascribed author of a poem in the *Theragāthā*.

Therī. An ascribed author of a poem in the *Therīgāthā*.

Vihāra. A building or complex of buildings in which Buddhist renunciants dwell; a monastery.

Vinaya. The formal code of rules for Buddhist renunciants.

INDEX